SCIENTIFIC AMERICAN EXPLORES BIG IDEAS

The Evolution of Medicine

Published in 2026 by Scientific American Educational Publishing
in association with **The Rosen Publishing Group**
2544 Clinton Street, Buffalo NY 14224

Contains material from Scientific American®, a division of Springer Nature America, Inc., reprinted by permission, as well as original material from The Rosen Publishing Group®.

First Edition

Scientific American
Lisa Pallatroni: Project Editor

Rosen Publishing
Michael Hessel-Mial: Compiling Editor
Michael Moy: Senior Graphic Designer

Cataloging-in-Publication Data

Names: Scientific American, Inc.
Title: The evolution of medicine / edited by the Scientific American Editors.
Description: Buffalo, New York : Scientific American Educational Publishing, an imprint of Rosen Publishing, 2026. | Series: Scientific American explores big ideas | Includes glossary and index.
Identifiers: ISBN 9781538313107 (pbk.) | ISBN 9781538313114 (library bound) | ISBN 9781538313121 (ebook)
Subjects: LCSH: Medicine–Forecasting–Juvenile literature. | Medical innovations–Juvenile literature. | Medical technology–Juvenile literature. | Medical care–Utilization–Juvenile literature.
Classification: LCC R130.5 E965 2026 | DDC 610.285–dc23

Manufactured in the United States of America
Websites listed were live at the time of publication.

Cover: nevodka/Shutterstock.com

CPSIA Compliance Information: Batch # CSSA26.
For Further Information contact Rosen Publishing at 1-800-237-9932.

CONTENTS

Introduction 5

Section 1: Ancient Medicine 6

1.1 Galen 7
By Frederick G. Kilgour

Section 2: Knowing the Human Body 14

2.1 Who Was Alessandra Giliani, 14th-Century Teen Anatomist? 15
By Katie Hafner

2.2 Vesalius: Discoverer of the Human Body 20
By Martin Gumpert

2.3 William Harvey 30
By Frederick G. Kilgour

Section 3: Curing Disease 38

3.1 Hidden Black Scientists Proved the Polio Vaccine Worked 39
By Ainissa Ramirez

3.2 AIDS in 1988 44
By Robert C. Gallo and Luc Montagnier

3.3 Cures for Sickle Cell Disease Arrive After a Painful Journey 57
By Maryn McKenna

Section 4: The Art of Surgery 69

4.1 Ambroise Paré 70
By Sir Geoffrey Keynes

4.2 The Late Joseph Lister: The Father of Antiseptic Surgery 76
By John B. Huber, A. M. , M. D.

Section 5: Medical Devices 82

5.1 The Medical Influence of the Stethoscope 83
By Stanley Joel Reiser

5.2 The Origins of Hypodermic Medication 93
By Norman Howard-Jones

Section 6: Sexual and Reproductive Health 105

6.1 Abortion and Contraception in the Middle Ages 106
By Roland Betancourt

6.2 The Forgotten History of the World's First Trans Clinic 111
By Brandy Schillace

6.3 The Disturbing History of Research into Transgender Identity 117
By Jack Turban

6.4 Commentary: The Eugenics Legacy of the Nobelist Who Fathered IVF 121
By Osagie K. Obasogie

Section 7: Public Health 127

7.1 Immunization against Smallpox before Jenner 128
By William L. Langer

7.2 What Florence Nightingale Can Teach Us about Architecture and Health 138
By Steven Lockley

7.3 We Learned the Wrong Lessons from the Tuskegee 'Experiment' 141
By Melba Newsome

7.4 In the Fight against Infectious Disease, Social Changes Are the New Medicine 144
By Maryn McKenna

Glossary 154

Further Information 156

Citations 157

Index 158

INTRODUCTION

Science is often considered a forward-thinking activity. Researchers want to make new discoveries and invent new things, especially to solve problems like sickness and injury. *Scientific American* often publishes such futuristic stories about the cutting edge. However, sometimes it's important to look back and see how our science has changed over the years. The articles in this title do just that for the field of medicine.

The opening chapter of this book explores one ancient medical scientist: Galen. Though his work is now out of date, he taught us some of the earliest research techniques. The chapters that follow explore key medical topics of anatomy, disease treatment, surgery, and medical devices. We'll find that practices and technologies we take for granted, like hand-washing, vaccines and stethoscopes, have fascinating histories. The final two chapters focus on two important subsets of medicine: reproductive/sexual health and public health.

When we look at the history of science, especially when people had ideas that were later proven incorrect, it's easy to see only the mistakes. However, often people who got some ideas wrong modeled the right way of asking questions and exploring data. In these stories, make sure to follow these older scientists' questions as well as their conclusions.

As you read, another important theme will emerge: Health is not just influenced by what's in the body, but the social world outside of the body. Many diseases in history have gone and continue to go untreated or unresearched because the people who suffer from them are mainly poor, women, or people of color. The scientists who look past their prejudices are often the ones who make discoveries that help everyone. This theme is especially important in public health, but appears in all of these chapters.

This book may not teach you about the most cutting-edge medical discovery of today, but by reading about the discoveries of yesterday, you'll have the tools to make the discoveries of tomorrow.

Section 1: Ancient Medicine

1.1 Galen
By Frederick G. Kilgour

Galen

By Frederick G. Kilgour

Galen of Pergamon towered above all other anatomists and physiologists of the ancient world. He established experimental physiology almost single-handed. Indeed, he ranks as one of the greatest experimental scientists in all history, certainly the foremost in ancient science. His life is also better known than that of any other ancient scientist, because his voluminous writings contain more autobiography than any other ancient Greek's.

Galen was born in 130 A.D. in or near Pergamon, about 50 miles due north of Smyrna in modern Turkey. His mother "was so irascible that she would sometimes bite her serving maids, and she was constantly shouting at my father and quarreling with him, worse than Xantippe with Socrates." In contrast his father Nicon stood out in his memory as "a most good-tempered, just, efficient and benevolent man." Nicon, a farmer, was no ordinary tiller of the soil but a cultured Greek, learned in geometry, arithmetic, architecture and astronomy. He conducted his son's education until the boy was nearly 15 and then sent him to study with various philosophers in Pergamon. When Galen was 17, Nicon had a dream indicating that his son should study medicine. Accordingly Galen studied anatomy with Satyrus in Pergamon for the next four years. His father died during this period and left Galen a bequest which made him practically independent financially for the rest of his life. The young man pursued the study of medicine and anatomy for seven more years in Smyrna, Corinth and Alexandria.

When, at the age of 28, Galen returned to Pergamon, the high priest of the medical temple, who was also the head of athletic games, appointed him physician for the gladiators-the equivalent of a present-day boxing commission doctor. In the brutal games of that time the athletes regularly incurred serious wounds. Galen evidently found the work interesting, for he served several years.

When war put an end to the games, he went to Rome to do research and practice medicine in the capital of the Empire. Galen was to spend the next 30 years of his life there, but in 167 he interrupted his stay and fled back to Pergamon because a great plague broke out in Rome. This apparent display of cowardice has been a matter of great controversy among his biographers. Today it would be most unethical for a physician to beat such a retreat. Apparently that was not the case in Galen's time, however, for he himself related the reason for his departure without embarrassment. In any case, he did not escape exposure to the plague. Not long after he left Rome for Pergamon the Emperor Marcus Aurelius summoned him back to the encampment of the Roman army at Aquileia, and Galen had no sooner arrived than the plague erupted among the soldiers. This time Galen saw the plague through, staying behind with the army after the Emperor left Aquileia and returned to Rome.

During his three decades in Rome Galen poured out an almost ceaseless stream of books and essays. A collection of his writings published in the early 19th century by C. G. Kühn ran to more than two and a half million words, and the collection was by no means complete. Galen lost some of his manuscripts in a fire which gutted Rome's Temple of Peace in 192, and in recent years scholars have discovered Arabic versions of previously missing publications, including part of his book *On Anatomical Procedures* and the entire text of *On Medical Experience*. There are undoubtedly still more to be uncovered. Galen divided his writings into two major groups: "those directed against swindlers" and the educational works on medical science. His polemics against "swindlers," which inveighed against human folly, have given Galen the reputation of being as bad-tempered as his mother. Actually he seems to have been a comparatively mild man–it was the time that was violent. He appears to have had few close friends, and he never married.

When Galen began his studies of anatomy and physiology, medicine was almost entirely innocent of a scientific basis. Hippocrates' initiation of rational medicine had been a *tour de force* founded only on shrewd observation, and the lesser men who followed him in the

500 years before Galen were split into squabbling sects, like the homeopaths, hydropaths, naturopaths, osteopaths, Thomsonians, Grahamites, etc., of the 19th century. Galen set out to develop systematic descriptions of the human body. He was handicapped by the fact that it was forbidden to dissect the dead. The only part of human anatomy that he could investigate in toto was the skeleton, which he often did "where tombs or monuments have been broken up." For the rest he relied on dissections of animals, including monkeys, and on examinations of tissues exposed in patients with disease or wounds. While he was studying with Satyrus at Pergamon, there was an epidemic of "carbuncle" (probably anthrax) which destroyed areas of skin and flesh in many of the victims. Galen wrote later: "Those of us who had seen Satyrus dissecting any of the denuded parts, easily recognized them and made a complete diagnosis, telling the patients to make some movement which we knew to be carried out by such and such a muscle, and sometimes diverting or drawing aside the muscles to observe an adjacent large artery, nerve or vein. We saw that all the other physicians were like blind men without any knowledge of the parts exposed."

Galen did not add a great deal to previous knowledge about the human bones, but he contributed hugely to knowledge of the muscles. He discovered many not previously recognized, and in all described about 300 muscles, some of which still bear the names he gave them. These were all muscles of the skeletal system: Galen put the involuntary muscles (of the heart, stomach and so on) in a separate category as "muscle-like" tissues. He was also confused about the attachment of the muscles, and mistakenly described the tendons as made up of nerves and ligaments.

Galen was the first to demonstrate that muscle has but one action–contraction. He proved by experiments that the movement of a muscle during its relaxation was produced by the contraction of an opposing muscle. He went on to establish that each muscle has only one direction of contraction. From the fact that the tongue can move in six different directions, anatomists had supposed that a muscle had various motions, but Galen dissected the tongue and found that it had at least as many muscles as directions of movement. His experiments in cutting muscles gave surgeons for the first time a sufficient understanding of muscular functions to realize what functions would be lost when muscles were cut through in surgery or were severed by a wound.

Attempting to discover what "force" caused muscles to contract, Galen came to the conclusion that the force originated in the brain and was communicated to the various muscles by the nerves. He arrived at this idea as a result of a wonderful series of experiments on the nervous system, particularly the spinal cord. Operating on experimental animals, he systematically cut the cord at one vertebra after the other down the backbone. He found that when he severed the cord between the first and second vertebrae in the neck, the animal instantly stopped breathing and died. Further down, the animal survived and retained certain functions. When he cut the cord between the sixth and seventh vertebrae, for instance, the chest muscles were paralyzed but the animal was able to breathe by means of its diaphragm. When he cut below the eighth vertebra, the arms escaped paralysis. He also observed that when the cord was cut only half way through, only one side of the body was paralyzed. In this way Galen mapped the control areas of the cord. In addition he investigated various peripheral nerves and established that in general the interruption of a nerve caused loss of motion and sensation below the block but not in the part of the body between it and the brain.

Galen's most celebrated work on the nervous system had to do with the nerves that control the movements of the vocal cords. These laryngeal nerves, two in number, are called "recurrent," because they start in the upper chest from the vagus nerve (coming from the brain), loop down under arteries not far from the heart and rise again through the chest and neck to the larynx. Galen discovered them accidentally one day while he was cutting nerves in the chest of a pig to observe disturbances of respiration. In the midst of the operation the pig suddenly stopped its squealing. (Galen later gave a public demonstration of this dramatic phenomenon.) He realized at once that he must have cut the nerves controlling the larynx, and he was able to trace the nerves via the vagus to the brain. One important result of this discovery was to settle an old controversy about the seat of intelligence. Hippocrates and others had placed it in the brain, but Aristotle had insisted it must lie in the heart, among other reasons because the voice seemed to originate from somewhere in the chest. Galen's discovery solved the problem by showing that the voice was actuated by nerves from the brain.

Galen proceeded to apply his new knowledge of the nervous system in seemingly hare-brained treatments which astounded his contemporaries. Pausanias, the Sophist, had lost sensation in three fingers of one hand. His physicians, after vainly trying to treat the hand for a month, called in Galen. Galen at once asked whether Pausanias had had a recent injury in the upper part of his body. Yes, he had tumbled out of his "car" on a stone and hurt the upper part of his back. Galen put applications on the area of the back injury, instead of on the hand, and Pausanias soon recovered feeling in his fingers.

The cure provoked a physiological argument between Galen and the other attending physicians. They maintained that if injury to a nerve from the spine were really the source of the trouble, the patient should have lost not only sensation but also the ability to move the fingers. But Galen replied, correctly, that the sensory and motor nerves had separate attachments to the cord. This was fully established in the 19th century by Sir Charles Bell and Francois Magendie; the Bell-Magendie law says that the anterior roots of spinal nerves are motor, and the posterior, sensory.

Galen developed a concept of the overall physiology of the body which sounds peculiar today and is often derided but which actually provided the seed from which modern ideas grew. He said that after food has been ingested into the alimentary tract, it passes through veins to the liver. That organ, he went on, changes the food into blood, imbued with "natural spirit." Most of the blood then goes to the right ventricle of the heart, entering it via the great vein, the *vena cava*. Galen knew that blood flows from the right ventricle to the lungs, through the pulmonary arteries. But lacking knowledge of the function of the lungs and of the heart-lung circulatory system, he had to explain how blood got into the main arterial system of the body. To make this event possible, he postulated that some of the blood in the right ventricle passed into the left ventricle through tiny pores in the wall between them. In the left ventricle the blood received "vital spirit" (coming from the lungs) and acquired a crimson color. The vitalized blood then was transmitted by the blood vessels to nourish all parts of the body. Blood reaching the brain took on "animal spirit," and the resulting concoction (which Galen never succeeded in detecting) went through the nerves.

If these ideas seem laughable, they become less so when we realize how radical a change in point of view they represented. Galen suggested a coherent idea of the functions and flow of the blood. He demonstrated by experiment that the arteries contain blood–not air, as some of his predecessors had believed–and he also established that the arteries and veins were connected in some way; he proved this by showing that when an animal's arteries were cut, the veins as well as the arteries became emptied of blood. Furthermore, with a few changes Galen's general concept of the body's physiology comes reasonably close to modern ideas. If we substitute oxygen for "vital spirit," and nerve electrical potential for "animal spirit," the system begins to approach a 20th-century description. Galen provided the foundation from which experimentalists during the last four centuries have developed present-day theories.

Galen returned to Pergamon in his sixties and devoted himself to writing, compiling two autobiographical books which he called *On the Series of My Books* and *On My Books.* He died in Pergamon about 200 A.D., at the age of 70 or so. Not for well over a thousand years did anyone approaching his stature in medicine arise in Europe. When, in 1543, Andreas Vesalius published the first of the great modern works on human anatomy, his work was based for the most part on Galen, though he corrected many of Galen's errors and added new observations. William Harvey's famous treatise on the circulation of the blood in 1628 also took its departure from Galen; indeed, he discussed Galen's experiments as if he were a contemporary. Fourteen hundred years after Galen the early modern investigators began to advance from the point where Galen had left off.

Section 2: Knowing the Human Body

2.1 Who Was Alessandra Giliani, 14th-Century Teen Anatomist?
By Katie Hafner

2.2 Vesalius: Discoverer of the Human Body
By Martin Gumpert

2.3 William Harvey
Frederick G. Kilgour

Who Was Alessandra Giliani, 14th-Century Teen Anatomist?

By Katie Hafner

Tulika Bose: Hey there, *Science, Quickly* listeners. I'm Tulika Bose, *Scientific American*'s senior multimedia editor. Today we're bringing you something we're sure you'll like–a new episode from our podcast partners, the *Lost Women of Science*. Their fabulous show recounts the remarkable stories of groundbreaking women who never got the full recognition they deserved–until now.

Today, they've brought us a fascinating story of a secret anatomist. Alessandra Giliani lived in the 14th century. That was 500 years before women were admitted to any medical school in the world. So Alessandra did what she had to to practice medicine. She put on a man's tunic and kirtle, snuck into the medical amphitheater and started dissecting cadavers.

Barbara Quick: There was a widely circulated story about this young girl, and the only way she could attend medical school in Italy at the time was to dress as a man.

Katie Hafner: I'm Katie Hafner, and this is *Lost Women of Science From Our Inbox*, a brand new series of mini episodes that you'll be hearing from now until, I'm not sure, maybe 2050. Because our list of women lost to history is long. On a regular basis, we're going to give you a brief burst of one woman's story that came to us from you, our listeners.

We're kicking off the series with an intriguing tip we received recently from Barbara Quick, a poet and novelist in the San Francisco Bay area. She wanted to tell us about Alessandra Giliani, a young woman who lived in Italy in the 14th century doing something unheard of: studying medicine.

If you don't find that stunning, consider this: most medical schools in the United States didn't start admitting women until 500 years later, around 1900, and Harvard Medical School had its first female graduates soon after World War II. So when the story of Alessandra Giliani floated into our inbox, we took notice.

Alessandra was thought to be an anatomist, dissecting human cadavers to better understand the body's internal systems and organs, and she did it in disguise. Quick's novel, *A Golden Web*, is a fictional account of Alessandra's life and work. *Lost Women of Science* associate producer Mackenzie Tatananni spoke with Barbara.

Barbara Quick: Alessandra was just 19 years old when she died, and it just makes me realize what a brief life this was, how consequential and how difficult to be someone as brilliant and precocious and determined as Alessandra was.

Mackenzie Tatananni: That's Barbara, telling the story as far as she knows it.

Barbara Quick: She lived, reputedly, 700 years ago, in San Giovanni in Persiceto and also in Bologna.

Mackenzie Tatananni: Barbara tells me that she stumbled upon Alessandra's story serendipitously.

Barbara Quick: I found her by accident in the course of looking into the life and work of another female anatomist who lived in Bologna 400 years later. But what happened when I turned up in Bologna and started doing my library research there was that I found evidence of another female anatomist, Alessandra Giliani, who died in the 1320s.

Mackenzie Tatananni: Barbara found evidence of Giliani's existence during a visit to a library in the town of San Giovanni in Persiceto in Northern Italy.

Barbara Quick: This librarian was able to let me examine these fantastic illuminated manuscripts of the time. And part of what they showed was the anatomy lessons given by Mondino de Luzzi.

And I saw clearly a young woman who was cross-dressed, who was assisting at the lessons. And as I looked into it more, I found that there was a widely circulated story that was written in the 18th century about this young girl who pursued medical school, and the only way she could attend medical school in Italy at the time was to dress as a man.

Mackenzie Tatananni: Dressed as a man. Giliani was believed to be a prosector, the person who does the cutting up of a cadaver during lecture demonstrations. Using a method of her own invention, she also challenged commonly held beliefs about the circulatory system.

Barbara Quick: For centuries, it was accepted as fact that blood passes from the right ventricle to the left ventricle of the heart through, quote unquote, "invisible pores in the septum."

Everyone believed that the heart itself was not a muscle and did not have a pumping function. The thought was that blood simply passed through it, which, of course, is completely wrong. The 17th century British medical researcher William Harvey, also at the University of Padua, is credited with finally setting the record straight about how the pulmonary circulatory system actually works.

Mackenzie Tatananni: But...

Barbara Quick: Written records from the 18th century chronicle the life and accomplishments of Alessandra Giliani, who reputedly carried out anatomical research that anticipated William Harvey's discoveries by some 300 years.

She developed a special system of making melted wax that was dyed. She used two colors, red and blue, to model the circulatory system. If it hadn't been against the laws of the Church and the government at the time for women to work in this capacity, many things would've changed and science would have progressed more quickly than it did.

Mackenzie Tatananni: Barbara Quick has reason to believe that the Church burned Giliani's work following her death, destroying nearly all traces of the young anatomist.

Barbara Quick: Somehow, if we had a time machine and could go back and give some kind of cloak of protection to Alessandra in her work, you know, who knows what she would've accomplished?

Mackenzie Tatananni: Yet one question continues to nag at historians. Did Giliani actually exist? Barbara Quick says, it's all a matter of choosing whose version of history you want to believe.

Barbara Quick: Well, you know, the most strident naysayers that I encountered in Italy in the medical historical community were all males. And I just think it's just that, you know, standard line about, oh, a woman couldn't have possibly done this.

Mackenzie Tatananni: But as we've learned, it is more than possible that a woman did this. And we'll just keep on researching and digging up their stories because there are plenty to tell. As we like to say at *Lost Women of Science*, we're not mad. We're curious.

Katie Hafner: And if you know of a female scientist who's been lost to history, go to our website to send us an email at lostwomenofscience.org. You'll also find the phone number to our tip line. We love getting calls to the tip line.

About the Author

Katie Hafner is host and co-executive producer of Lost Women of Science. She was a longtime reporter for the New York Times, *where she remains a frequent contributor. Hafner is uniquely positioned to tell these stories. Not only does she bring a skilled hand to complex narratives, but she has been writing about women in STEM for more than 30 years. She is also host and executive producer of* Our Mothers Ourselves, *an interview podcast, and the author of six nonfiction books. Her first novel,* The Boys, *was published by Spiegel & Grau in July. Follow Hafner on Twitter @katiehafner.*

Vesalius: Discoverer of the Human Body

By Martin Gumpert

On July 17, 1903, in Baltimore, young Harvey Cushing received the following post card from the Isle of Guernsey: "I have bagged two 1543 *Fabricas*! 'Tis not a work to be left on the shelves of a bookseller." The card was signed by the great physician William Osler. A week later came another message: "Besides the two '43 *Fabricas* I have just ordered a third. We cannot have too many copies in America & no medical library is complete without one."

By autumn the three copies had grown to six, among them an imperfect first edition discovered in a Rome blacksmith's shop by another of Cushing's peripatetic friends. When Osler returned to Baltimore, the two bibliophiles spread their loot on his dining room table. It was a solemn and happy moment. From the obscurity that sometimes attends greatness, the two friends had retrieved six first editions of a treatise which Osler called "the greatest medical work ever printed."

Osler distributed his precious volumes to medical libraries with missionary enthusiasm. For Cushing, the moment in Osler's dining room was the beginning of a lifelong labor of love. His copy of the *Fabrica* grew into the world's most complete collection of works by its author, Andreas Vesalius. It is now in the Historical Library of the School of Medicine at Yale University. Today one need not hunt abroad for a copy of the *Fabrica*. The New York Academy of Medicine has even sponsored the publication of a modern edition from the original Vesalius woodcuts.

This sixteenth century work, *De Humani Corporis Fabrica*, written by the founder of modern anatomy, is indeed one of the most daring, creative and beautiful adventures ever undertaken by the human spirit. No one who can be moved by genius should die without seeing it. For medical men, whose work so often leads to a final attitude of cynicism, it has the power to turn cynicism into enthusiasm. It is regrettable that all young doctors are not made familiar with the life and work of Vesalius. This, however, is an unhappy by-product of the fact that even the best medical schools neglect the teaching of medical history. The anatomy textbook of today is a medical Sears Roebuck catalogue. The anatomy of Vesalius is a testament of passionate devotion to medicine. Any doctor who has made the acquaintance of this powerful book will be better prepared for the practice of medicine and its deep and dangerous beauty.

The *Fabrica* is more than a milestone in the history of medicine. It is a great work of creative art. Curiously, it is not notable for literary quality. "As a book," Cushing once observed, "the *Fabrica* has probably been more admired and less read than any publication of equal significance in the history of science." But its text, like the libretto of an opera, has become merely scaffolding for the great music of its illustrations.

These illustrations depict man's first clear and accurate knowledge of human anatomy. Even now, after four centuries, the *Fabrica*'s drawings show the freshness and enthusiasm of original discovery. In its perfect unity of format, print, picture and scholarship, the *Fabrica* is comparable to the great creations of early religious literature. Indeed, its perfection could have been achieved only through a reverence for the exquisite architecture of the human body.

The book was the joint product of a scientist–one whom Cushing ranked with Hippocrates, Galen, Harvey and Lister among the five great discoverers in medicine–and an artist, Jan Stephan van Calcar. A pupil of Titian, Calcar drew the anatomical features which Vesalius laid bare.

Great books and great discoveries are always dangerous, and the *Fabrica* was no exception. It was as daring as the later heresies of Galileo. It radically revised concepts of the structure of the human body which men had been taught for centuries. In its precise identification of all the organs, it seemed to leave no room for the "seat of the soul"–a perilous omission. The fury of the attack launched against the *Fabrica* was not reduced by the circumstance that Vesalius was only 28 when it was published.

Vesalius was a Belgian, born in Brussels on December 31, 1514. He came of a long line of illustrious physicians. His great-grandfather was doctor to Maximilian I of Burgundy. Grandfather Eberhard wrote a commentary on a famous textbook by Rhazes, the renowned medieval Arab physician. Vesalius' father was apothecary to Emperor Charles V of the Holy Roman Empire.

Vesalius' interest in anatomy began early. As a boy he dissected mice, moles, cats and dogs. These experiences possibly are reflected in the drawings of fat little cherubs performing dissections which decorate the initial letters of the *Fabrica*'s chapters. By the time he had begun his medical studies at the University of Louvain, and soon afterward in Paris, his interest had become a passion. He obtained his first skeleton by robbing a gibbet.

Vesalius' ardor for dissection did not please his instructors. In the sixteenth century it was regarded as indecent for a professor to take a knife in his own hand for dissection. At lectures this odious task was performed by barber surgeons. Vesalius reported of his teacher Guenther von Andernach, known as Guinterius, that he never saw him with a knife in his hand except at the dinner table.

The earnest young scientist soon became impatient with his teachers. Instruction in anatomy consisted of lectures, an occasional glimpse of a butchered dog and an annual dissection of a human corpse by the rude, ignorant hands of the barbers. Never did he see a nerve, an artery, a vein; never did he dare to take a bone in his hand.

So Vesalius began his own independent study of anatomy. He prowled about Paris churchyards and places of execution for subjects. At the cemetery of St. Innocent and at Montfaucon, dumping ground for the bodies of criminals, he was a constant visitor. Sometimes he fought with wild dogs for the corpses he dragged home to dissect in the quiet of his room. Soon he could recognize every bone with his eyes closed, just by touching it. His skill gained him the privilege of acting as the barber at demonstrations. While he was still a student at Louvain he shocked his teachers by conducting a demonstration in which he lectured and dissected at the same time. It was the first public dissection at the university in 18 years.

At 22, Vesalius escaped this barren environment for the stimulating intellectual atmosphere of Venice. In this period Venice was the focus of the Catholic revival. Amid contrasts of luxury and pestilence, culture and filth, the serenity of Greek theology and groans of hunger, the Renaissance was drawing to a close. Vesalius threw his useful talents into the crusade of brotherly love launched by Ignatius Loyola and his new order of Jesuits. He helped the Jesuits care for the dying, the prisoners and the lepers. He bled patients, set leeches to work and tested the wonderful healing powers of quinine, recently brought from Peru by sailors.

Presently, just before his 23rd birthday, Vesalius was appointed professor of surgery and anatomy at the University of Padua. Now he had the means to realize his great dream–to get on with the science of anatomy. He began at once to reorganize the system of instruction. One of his first ventures was a full-dress public dissection. From all over Europe, hundreds of physicians, philosophers and theologians came to see and hear his demonstration. It lasted for three weeks of all-day sessions. Vesalius dissected dogs and other animals, displayed sections of human anatomy and climaxed his lecture by exhibiting a complete human skeleton.

In the midst of the revolutionary sixteenth century, anatomy was still dominated by the second century Greek physician Galen. European medicine, emerging from the medieval spell of Arabian science, was on the crest of a surge of neo-Galenism. The revival, moreover, was led by two of Vesalius' old teachers–Guinterius and Jacobus Sylvius, the latter the most renowned medical lecturer in Europe. Vesalius himself, as he began his work at Padua, was still a loyal Galenist.

But already Vesalius had begun to discover errors which had been committed by the master. His dissections showed, for example, that the actual course of the azygos vein, running up through the diaphragm to the vena cava, was entirely different from Galen's description. As a result, Vesalius published a little treatise called *Letters on Vein-Cutting*, suggesting a new blood-letting procedure based on his discovery. This work was shortly followed by Vesalius' first anatomical publication, an outline of his lectures which he called *Tabulae Analomicae*. It is fascinating to study these first anatomical sketches of Vesalius–three drawn by himself and three by Calcar. The correction of Galen's errors is already under way. But some glaring ones still remain: the liver is still shown with five lobes, the breastbone still has seven parts, the uterus is shaped like a bubble, the heart is inaccurately sketched, the pelvis is falsely situated.

Vesalius did not yet dare to challenge Galen's basic anatomy. He hunted assiduously but vainly for organs which Galen had mentioned. The plexus mirabilis, which Galen had described in minute detail, he could find in sheep but not in man. Then, in the year 1540, Vesalius was enlisted in a project which was to become the turning point of his studies. This was the translation of Galen's collected works into a magnificent new Latin edition. Vesalius edited the parts on the dissection of the nerves and blood vessels, especially one of Galen's most important works, *De Anatomicis Administrationibus*.

As he worked on this translation, Vesalius was delivering a course of lectures at Bologna, during which he reconstructed the skeletons of a man and a monkey. When the work was finished, he compared the two. In the monkey he found a lumbar vertebral process which was described in Galen's anatomy but which apparently did not exist in the human skeleton.

A great revelation dawned upon Vesalius. He realized, with sudden, shocking perception. that Galen had never dissected the human body. Galen's anatomy was that of the ape! The obscure and erroneous details that had bothered him for years were cleared up at a stroke. His long, frustrating search for the imaginary organs mentioned by Galen was at an end. Vesalius' reaction to his astonishing discovery was characteristic: he was ashamed of himself. He wrote: "*Ipse meam stupidi, tatem et nimiam in Galeni aliorumque Anatomicorum scriptis fidem haud satis demirari possum*"–"I could not get over wondering at my own stupidity and overconfidence in Galen and the writings of the other anatomists."

That day in 1540 marked the birth of modern anatomy. Vesalius now went to work to present the first accurate description of the structure of the human body. It took him only two years to complete the *Fabrica*. Meanwhile, he also undertook the dangerous task of removing Galen from his shrine in scientific opinion. His public dissections took on the character of turbulent mass meetings. He was greeted with both praise and bitterness as he destroyed the legend of Galen by citing more than 200 errors in his anatomy. "Thou, Galen," he declaimed, "who hast been betrayed by thine apes!"

On August 1, 1542 his work was finished. He took the huge manuscript to Venice and shipped it, with all the woodcuts and minutely detailed directions, to his publisher Oporinus in Basel. Vesalius soon followed to supervise the printing personally. But even while attending the birth of his masterpiece, he went on with his dissections. On May 12, 1543, a criminal named Jakob Karrer was beheaded. Vesalius promptly seized upon his body to perform the first dissection that had been witnessed in Basel in 12 years. For four centuries the skeleton Vesalius constructed from the bones has outlasted Jakob Karrer's misdeeds, whatever they were. Today it is still treasured by the Vesalianum in Basel as the oldest preserved anatomical specimen in the world.

In June of 1543 the great book finally appeared. Actually it was two books. Besides the exhaustive *Fabrica*, Latin and German editions of an *Epitome* were published for laymen. This was an outline of the new science and a safeguard against unauthorized condensations and translations.

In the woodcut which appears on the first page of the *Fabrica* one may see a portrait of Vesalius at 28–a bold, eager man with curly hair, piercing eyes, a high forehead, an upturned nose and a small birthmark over the right eyebrow. On the table before him are the flexor muscles of a cadaver's right forearm laid bare. Vesalius, grasping the hand, is supposedly exhibiting one of Galen's errors.

The frontispiece of the *Fabrica*, a panoramic view of Vesalius' dissection theater, boldly symbolizes his defiance of tradition and his devotion to science. At the center, Vesalius, scalpel in hand, stands beside a table upon which lies a woman's nude body with the viscera laid open. Every detail in the picture is a deliberate rebuke to the academicians. At the conventional medical lectures of the time the professor sat high on a kind of throne, reading a chapter from Galen. Below, the demonstrator, a physician, pointed with a wooden staff at the organs to which the reading referred. Even lower, in the pit of the theater, the barbers cut up the body, or rather, hacked at it with clumsy hands. In the *Fabrica* a skeleton occupies the throne of the professor, while Vesalius stands and lectures in the midst of his students. Underneath the table two squatting barbers disconsolately brandish their razors. Flanking the picture at the bottom are an ape and a dog—the rejected subjects of traditional dissections. At the left, braced against a column, is a naked figure which illustrates the play of living muscles. The bearded figure at the right, directing a servant to quiet the dog, is believed to be Realdus Colombo, Vesalius' assistant. At the top of the picture, upheld by naked little angels of anatomy, is Vesalius' family coat of arms–three fleeing weasels. And packing the theater to the doors is a throng of fascinated students, watching the dramatic event with the taut faces of men trembling with excitement.

The frontispiece falls short of being an artistic masterpiece, but it is a masterful illustration of Vesalius' place in the history of medicine. This is the birth of anatomy, firm foundation of the art of healing and of all scientific investigation of the human body.

The principal illustrations of the *Fabrica* are its anatomical drawings, imprinted on folio pages by woodcuts. These fall into a narrative which unfolds like a great voyage of discovery. Calcar's massive figures are almost supernatural beings, each animated by an intellect. In attitudes of monumental suffering, their giant forms rise from a continuous landscape, identified as a section of Petrarch's countryside in the Euganean Hills near Padua. From page to page the giants shed their muscles like tall trees shedding their leaves in autumn, the landscape suffering with them. The narrative proceeds with the structure of great drama: in the final pages the figures stand on naked rock, stripped of every connection with life–poor remnants of humanity sinking on their knees, leaning against a wall or hung up by cords. From this has the study of anatomy sunk to a mere pedantic exercise!

The *Fabrica* was to revolutionize surgery and to found a new era of physiology from which was to grow the discipline of modern medicine. But it broke upon its time like the first nuclear chain reaction. Vesalius' old professor, Sylvius, called him a "madman," an unprincipled upstart who had disgraced his teaching. Guinterius turned against him. Even Vesalius' assistant, Colombo, a gifted but unscrupulous careerist, did his best to discredit him in his own stronghold of Padua.

Vesalius lacked the toughness that often accompanies genius. The attacks discouraged him. Within a year, during a fit of depression, he burned most of his notes and scientific papers and fled his university and his science. He began an entirely new life as court physician to Charles V in Madrid. He accompanied the emperor on military campaigns and to conferences throughout Europe. He also married Anna van Hamme, the daughter of a royal councillor in Brussels. In his bitter *Letter on China-Root* (quinine), which be wrote to a friend, he exclaimed: "Never again will I procure scientific material for myself and my pupils with such labor and danger as once I did in Paris, Louvain and Italy. In my youthful enthusiasm for science I endured this willingly and easily. Now I am through with the passion for writing." Vesalius was 31.

In 1556 his life took a minor turn. When Charles V gave his throne to his son Philip II, Vesalius entered Philip's service in Spain. This was probably the period when the portrait of Vesalius ascribed to Titian–now in Florence's Palazzo Pitti–was painted. It shows Vesalius with thinning hair and the high, pale forehead of a man growing old. A graying, slightly ruffled beard melts into the enormous breadth of his heavy body. His right hand holds a pair of spectacles. His left holds a book, an index finger between the pages. His wise, resigned eyes gaze past the beholder over some melancholy vista. It is Vesalius–without goals, lost in the darkness and corruption of the Spanish empire.

But the last spark had not quite been extinguished. While he was in Spain Vesalius received a book entitled *Observationes*

Anatomicae, by Gabriele Falloppio, whose name is commemorated by the Fallopian tubes. Falloppio of Modena had been through an early career much like that of Vesalius. At 24 he was a professor in Ferrara, and he succeeded to Vesalius' chair in Padua after the treacherous Colombo resigned. In a clear, forthright script, every line of which breathed respect, Falloppio advised Vesalius of a few errors in the *Fabrica*, described the organs of hearing and gave an exact anatomy of the uterus, the ovaries and the clitoris.

For Vesalius, Falloppio's manuscript was a trumpet call. He read it in a fever of interest and in a few days wrote his last work, *Comment on Falloppio*. He sent the manuscript to Falloppio, but before it could be delivered Falloppio had died. Vesalius' book was published two years later in Venice.

In the spring of 1564 Vesalius set out on a pilgrimage to Jerusalem, from which he was not to return alive. The reason for this journey and the circumstances of his death have never been completely clarified. According to a letter written by a Paris physician in 1565, Vesalius had a distinguished patient in Spain who died of an unknown sickness. "When he believed him dead," wrote the Parisian. "he asked the relatives for permission to perform an autopsy. This was granted, but when he opened the chest, the heart was still beating. The relatives accused Vesalius of manslaughter and Godlessness before the Inquisition. Since the killing was proved, the Inquisition wanted to sentence him to death. Only with difficulty was the king able to free him from great danger. Finally he was released on condition that for the expiation of his crime he should go on a pilgrimage to Jerusalem and Mount Sinai."

On Vesalius' return journey from Jerusalem, according to another report, his ship was wrecked on Zante, one of the Ionian Islands to the west of Greece. There he lay dying, untouched by the inhabitants because they thought he was a victim of the plague. Shortly before he died he was found on the beach by a visiting Venetian goldsmith. There, at 50, Vesalius was buried in an unmarked grave. If this account may be accepted, there is a strange parallel between the end of Vesalius and the end of his great book. On the last page of the *Fabrica* is a concluding illustration, said to have been chosen by Vesalius himself. It is a picture of Arion, the poet and musician of Lesbos, who during a voyage was robbed and driven into the sea by Corinthian sailors. Vesalius had almost predicted his own death, and had chosen his monument.

About the Author

Martin Gumpert is a practicing physician and a writer on medical subjects.

William Harvey

By Frederick G. Kilgour

> *And I remember that when I asked our famous Harvey, in the only Discourse I had with him, (which was but a while before he dyed). What were the things that induc'd him to think of a* Circulation of the Blood? *He answer'd me, that when he took notice that the Valves in the Veins of so many several Parts of the Body, were so Plac'd that they gave free passage to the Blood Towards the Heart, but oppos'd the passage of the Venal Blood the Contrary way: He was invited to imagine, that so Provident a Cause as Nature had not so Plac'd so many Valves without design: and no Design seem'd more probable than that, since the Blood could not well, because of the interposing Valves, be sent by the Veins to the Limbs; it should be sent through the Arteries, and Return through the Veins, whose Valves did not oppose its course that way.*

The Irish chemist Robert Boyle reported this interview with William Harvey in his *Disquisition about Final Causes of Natural Things*, published 31 years after Harvey's death. It is the only recorded statement from Harvey of the clue that led him to his great discovery—an Alpine peak in the history of biology. This man who laid the basis of modern medicine is hardly known today except as a name. His classic work, written in Latin and titled *Exercitatio Anatomica de Motu Cordis et Sanguinis in Animalibus* (*Anatomical Studies on the Motion of the Heart and Blood in Animals*), is widely celebrated but little read. Both the man and the work are actually much more interesting than their conspicuous obscurity might suggest.

"Our famous Harvey" was born of yeoman stock at Folkestone in 1578; his father later became mayor of the city. Harvey was a schoolboy of 10 when the Spanish Armada sailed against England; he set up practice as a physician in London in the last year of Elizabeth's reign; he gave his first lecture on the circulation of the blood in 1616, the year that Shakespeare died. Like Shakespeare,

Harvey left us his works but not very much about himself. Most of our knowledge about his person and character derives from the librarian and biographer John Aubrey, who wrote a "Brief Life" on him. Harvey, says Aubrey, was a very short man with a "little eie [eye], round, very black, full of spirit." He was temperamental and had his eccentricities. As a young blood he wore a dagger in the fashion of the day and was wont to draw it on slight provocation. It is a matter of record that he married at the age of 26, but nothing is known about his wife or family life, except that he had no children. In his later years (he lived to the age of 79) Harvey liked to be in the dark, because he could think better, and he had underground caves constructed at his house in Surrey for meditation.

Harvey is known to have been a copious scribbler. He wrote hastily, and all but illegibly, in a mixture of Latin and English, and was a careless speller: in one place in his notes appears the word "piggg"–an unusually liberal number of "g's" even for 17th-century English. Aside from his classic *De Motu Cordis*, few of his writings survive. One reason is that he lost many of his papers during the Civil War of 1642, when rioters looted his house in London and destroyed his manuscripts while he was away in Nottingham with Charles I, to whom Harvey was Physician-in-Ordinary. Harvey later said this loss was the most crucifying he had ever experienced.

A dynamic little man, he spent his life in the ardent pursuit of learning, and he wrote at least a dozen treatises on various subjects, but these, like the manuscripts destroyed by the looters, were never published and none is now known to exist. Of his few published works perhaps the most important, next to *De Motu Cordis*, was *De Generatione* (*On Reproduction*) , which made several valuable contributions to embryology.

His work on the circulation of the blood remains, however, his one great monument. It was remarkable not only as a history-making discovery but as a pioneering expression of the scientific method in biology. Harvey was a contemporary of Galileo, Kepler, Bacon and Descartes. The scientific revolution of the Renaissance, which swept away the systems of classical philosophy and established the methods upon which modern science is based, found in him one of its earliest prodigies. Harvey was the first biologist to use quantitative methods to demonstrate an important discovery. To weigh, to measure, to count and thus to arrive at truth was such a new idea in the 17th century that even a man of Harvey's genius could do it only badly. But his application of quantitative procedures to biology ushered in the modern age for that science.

Harvey graduated from Cambridge University in 1597 and went to study medicine at the University of Padua, the greatest scientific school of the day. The anatomy and physiology of the heart, arteries, veins and blood then being taught was still mainly the system that had been constructed 14 centuries earlier by the Greek physician Galen. According to Galen, chyle (a kind of lymph) passed from the intestines to the liver, which converted it to venous blood and at the same time added a "natural spirit." The liver then distributed this blood through the venous system, including the right ventricle of the heart. Galen knew from experiment that when he severed a large vein or artery in an animal, blood would drain off from both the veins and the arteries. He realized, therefore, that there must be some connection between the veins and the arteries, and he believed he had found such a connection in the form of pores in the wall dividing the left side of the heart from the right. He argued that the venous blood oozed through these supposed pores to the left heart, was there charged with *vital spirit* coming from the lungs and thus took on the bright crimson color of arterial blood. According to the Galenic scheme, blood flowed to various parts of the body through both the veins and the arteries to supply the body members with nourishment and spirit. There was no real circulation or motive power; the blood in the vessels simply ebbed back occasionally to the heart and lungs for the removal of impurities.

To Galen's scheme two important modifications had been made by Harvey's time. Andreas Vesalius of Padua, the founder of modern anatomy, had announced in 1555 that Galen's "pores" did not exist, and Vesalius' successor Realdo Colombo had discovered the system whereby the blood flows from the right side of the heart through the pulmonary arteries to the lungs and thence via the pulmonary veins to the left side of the heart. He showed by animal experiments that the pulmonary veins contain arterial blood, not "vital spirit." The second important discovery, made by Fabricius ab Aquapendente at Padua, had been that the veins possess valves–"little doors," he called them. Fabricius did not realize their function; he suggested, following Galen's ideas, that they were designed to slow the flow of blood into the extremities.

Harvey, with his doctor's degree from Padua, returned to England in 1602. Whether or not he had begun to form his notion of the circulation of the blood when he left Padua we do not know. In any event, he proceeded to practice medicine in London and rose rapidly in his profession. In 1615 the Royal College of Physicians, of which he was a fellow, honored him with the lifetime post of Lumleian Lecturer. In his first series of Lumleian lectures, given in 1616, he began to describe the circulation of the blood. We have his 98-page set of notes outlining these lectures. In them he describes some of his experiments, including the one which satisfied him "that so Provident a Cause as Nature had not Plac'd so many Valves without design" and which gave him the idea of the circulation, as he later told Robert Boyle.

The notes make clear that Harvey was already convinced that the blood circulates through the body and that the heart is its pumping engine. He concluded his 1616 series of lectures with this statement:

> *It is proved by the structure of the heart that the blood is continuously transferred through the lungs into the aorta, as by two clacks of a water bellows to raise water. It is proved by the ligature that there is a passage of blood from the arteries to the veins. It is therefore demonstrated that the continuous movement of the blood in a circle is brought about by the beat of the heart. Is this for the sake of nutrition, or the better preservation of the blood and members by the infusion of heat, the blood in turn being cooled by heating the members and heated by the heart?*

Twelve years later Harvey, having carried out further experiments to prove his circulation theory, published *De Motu Cordis*. It is a book of only 72 pages. The volume contains two dedications (to King Charles and to Doctor Argent, President of the Royal College), an introduction and 17 brief chapters presenting his arguments.

After giving in Chapter I his reasons for writing the book (among them the desire to protect himself from ridicule), Harvey devoted the next four chapters to a remarkable analysis of the movements of the heart, arteries and auricles and an equally remarkable analysis of the functions of the heart. He had despaired at first of ever understanding the movement of the heart in warm-blooded animals, because its pulsation was so rapid, but he had found that he could analyze heart motions in cold-blooded animals and in dying warm-blooded ones. So far as direct inspection is concerned, such observations are still our principal sources for knowledge of heart motion.

Harvey gave the first clear statement of the apex beat, of the muscular character of the heart, and of the origin of the heartbeat in the right auricle and its conduction to the other auricle and the ventricles. He also demonstrated that the pulse in the arteries is due to the impact of blood ejected by the heart, as when "one blows into a glove," an image he used first in his 1616 lectures. Harvey correctly concluded that "the principal function of the heart is the transmission and pumping of the blood through the arteries to the extremities of the body."

He went on to review the movement of the blood from the right side of the heart through the lungs to the left side of the heart, as Colombo had described it, and to demonstrate how the blood passes from the left heart through the arteries to the extremities and thence via the veins back to the right heart. This section of the book contains the core of Harvey's discovery. He employed three "propositions" to prove that the blood must circulate: 1) the amount of blood transmitted from the veins to the arteries is so great that all the blood in the body must pass through the heart in a short time; this quantity could not be produced by the food consumed, as Galen held; 2) the amount of blood going to the extremities is much greater than needed for the nutrition of the body; 3) the blood continuously returns to the heart from the extremities through the veins.

It was to prove the first proposition that Harvey engaged in his famous quantitative work–the determination of the volume of blood pumped by the heart. To make this calculation, he had to measure the amount of blood that the heart ejects with each beat and to establish the pulse rate. The measurement of cardiac output is a tough problem, and even today there are wide variations in the measurements obtained by the various methods. But Harvey got a figure that is only one-eighteenth of the lowest estimate used today. How could he have arrived at such a ridiculously incorrect figure and at the same time have used it successfully to demonstrate such an important discovery?

Harvey based his reckoning on the fact that in a cadaver he once examined the left ventricle of the heart held more than two ounces of blood. (It must have been a dilated heart.) He assumed that between contractions the ventricle might hold as little as an ounce and a half. Assuming further that the ventricle with each contraction ejects "a fourth, a fifth, sixth or only an eighth" of its contents (we now think it ejects nearly all), he finally calculated that the cardiac output must be at least 3.9 grams per beat. According to a present-day estimate, it is actually in the neighborhood of 89 grams. Harvey can certainly be excused for not obtaining any close estimate of the output of the human heart, but he got virtually as poor results when he tried to measure the output of a sheep's heart. If he had severed a sheep's aorta and weighed the amount of blood ejected in one minute while counting the heartbeats for that minute, he could have obtained a reasonably accurate figure for cardiac output in sheep. But he never performed that obvious experiment.

Harvey also missed the mark widely in his other important measurement–the pulse rate. Somehow he counted it to be 33 per minute, about half the actual average rate, and although he obtained other values, he generally used this figure. We cannot explain this error on the ground that it is a difficult measurement to make; why he went so wrong will always be a mystery. With his two estimates–3.9 grams for cardiac output and 33 pulse beats per minute–he obtained a figure for the rate of blood flow which is one-36th of the lowest value accepted today. One of his calculations reads: "In half an hour the heart will make 1,000 beats, in some as many as two, three, and even four thousand. Multiplying the number of drams ejected by the number of beats there will be in half an hour either 3,000 drams, 2,000 drams, 500 ounces or some proportionate quantity of blood transferred into the arteries by the heart, but always a larger quantity than is contained in the whole body." In this summation, the lowest weight, 2,000 drams, equals 17.1 pounds, which is well in excess of the total of 15 pounds of blood contained by an average human body weighing 150 pounds.

Even with his faulty calculations, Harvey proved his main point: that each half-hour the blood pumped by the heart far exceeds the total weight of blood in the body. This was a blow to the Galenic concept, for it was obvious that the food a man eats could not produce blood continuously in any such volume.

Less impressive was Harvey's demonstration of the second proposition: that the amount of blood going to the extremities is much greater than is needed for the nutrition of the body. He used no specific measurements and argued largely by inference. However, in this discussion he made the important point that the blood must pass from the arteries to the veins in the extremities. And he described here the experiment that had first suggested the circulation idea. By employing a bandage in such a way as to stop the flow in the veins while leaving the arteries open, he showed that the veins would swell but not the arteries. When he increased pressure enough to cut off the arteries as well, the veins did not swell. From these observations, Harvey reasoned correctly that the blood entered the extremities through the arteries and passed somehow to the veins. He later looked for the channels of connection but could not find them.

By another historic experiment Harvey proved his third proposition: that the blood flows in the veins toward the heart and not away from it, as the Galenic concept held. He showed that if one pressed a finger on a vein and moved the finger along the vein from below one valve to above the next, the blood thus pushed up the vein did not return to the emptied section. In short, the valves were one-way; the blood did not flow back and forth in the venous system.

What are the principal features of Harvey's discovery? The essential factors of the cardiovascular system which effect the circulation of the blood are the pumping heart, the passage of the blood from one side of the heart through the lungs to the other side and its subsequent passage through the arteries to every part of the body and back through the veins to the heart again. Harvey already knew of the passage through the lungs when he began his work; his great contribution was to demonstrate the circulation through the arteries and veins and to integrate it with the pulmonary passage, thus establishing one comprehensive system for the movement of blood through the body. There remained, of course, one final uncharted link: How did the blood pass from the arteries to the veins in the extremities in order to return to the heart? Thirty-three years after the appearance of *De Motu Cordis* the Italian anatomist Marcello Malpighi filled in that link by discovering the capillaries and so completed Harvey's scheme.

The direct contributions of Harvey's discovery to medicine and surgery are obviously beyond measuring: it is the basis for all work in the repair of damaged or diseased blood vessels, the surgical treatment of high blood pressure and coronary disease, the well-known "blue baby" operation, and so on. It is general physiology, however, that is most in his debt. For the notion of the circulating blood is what underlies our present understanding of the self-stabilizing internal environment of the body. In the dynamics of the human system the most important role is played by the fluid whose circulation Harvey discovered by a feat of great insight.

About the Author

Frederick G. Kilgour is librarian of the Yale Medical Library.

Section 3: Curing Disease

3.1 Hidden Black Scientists Proved the Polio Vaccine Worked
By Ainissa Ramirez

3.2 AIDS in 1988
By Robert C. Gallo and Luc Montagnier

3.3 Cures for Sickle Cell Disease Arrive After a Painful Journey
By Maryn McKenna

Hidden Black Scientists Proved the Polio Vaccine Worked

By Ainissa Ramirez

In the summers of the early 1950s, multitudes of American children were stuck in their home. Parents didn't permit them to play together because, when the weather got warm, society entered a nightmare called polio. Children would eagerly begin their school breaks with a bicycle, scooter or kite and end them in crutches, braces or an iron lung.

The disease poliomyelitis, or polio, had been in the medical textbooks for decades. In the summers of the early 20th century, however, this illness grew into an epidemic. The virus behind the disease could infect anyone, but in the U.S., it caused the worst damage among children under five years old, and polio was consequently called infantile paralysis.

In early 1953 there was a glimmer of hope that this nightmare might come to an end. Medical researcher Jonas Salk created a polio vaccine that, when injected, stimulated the immune system to make antibodies that fought off the virus. By January of that year, he had inoculated 161 people, and the results looked promising. Salk's work was funded by the National Foundation for Infantile Paralysis (NFIP). This organization–founded in 1938 by polio sufferer and U.S. president Franklin Delano Roosevelt–evolved from a dilapidated spa in Warm Springs, Ga., for those afflicted with the disease to become a major polio research funder. Buoyed by Salk's early results, the NFIP, with its broad mission of conquering polio, started pushing to get hundreds of thousands of children vaccinated. But before moving ahead, Salk wanted to make sure his vaccine was the "safest and most certain" approach by monitoring the inoculation's ability to trigger enough antibodies to neutralize the virus. In earlier tests, monkeys were injected with the vaccine and monitored to see if they got sick, or their cells were observed to see if they deformed. But the number of the animals needed to test thousands of children was too costly and cumbersome.

Fortunately, researchers had found there were unique cells that could help. These were HeLa cells, the living line of cancer cells that were taken without permission from a Black patient named Henrietta Lacks years earlier. After blood was drawn from a vaccinated patient, part of it was placed in a glass dish along with HeLa cells and a small dose of polio. With those items, a microscopic–and deadly–battle commenced. In the dish, the poliovirus tried to attack the HeLa cells. If there were enough of the proper antibodies in the patient's blood, however, they blocked the virus from causing any harm. Scientists could readily see the cells under a microscope. If the HeLa cells looked misshapen, this meant that the right antibodies were not present in the blood.

To evaluate his vaccine, Salk would need tremendous amounts of HeLa cells. He would get help not from traditional established institutions such as Harvard University or Yale University but from a small Black college in the South that had become famous for cultivating peanuts. In 1881 educator Booker T. Washington founded the Tuskegee Institute with 30 pupils inside an old church building in Alabama. Washington had big dreams for his small school, and they were realized. Just 50 years later, the number of students increased 100-fold. And the entire nation grew to know about this institute from botanist George Washington Carver's pioneering work on cultivating the peanut there. During World War II, the Tuskegee Airmen, an all-Black flying squadron, also put this sleepy part of the country on the map.

The NFIP had an old relationship with the Tuskegee Institute. In the 1940s, the NFIP funded the Tuskegee Infantile Paralysis Center, which not only supported the treatment of Black polio sufferers but also trained Black medical personnel for work back in their communities. This medical facility was one of the few polio centers that treated Black children because American hospitals were segregated. Even FDR's Warm Springs did not accept Black patients. In October 1952, looking ahead to polio vaccine testing, the NFIP's director of research, Harry Weaver, asked Russell W. Brown, director of the Carver Research Foundation at the Tuskegee Institute, to turn its halls into the world's first HeLa cell factory. Brown, who had a doctorate in bacterial physiology, was designated as the director of the project, and James (Jimmy) Henderson, a plant physiologist, assisted him. These Black men were asked to serve humanity in a time when their humanity was often denied. Not far from them, the infamous Tuskegee syphilis experiment was underway.

Both Brown and Henderson were solid scientists, but growing, storing and maintaining HeLa cells had not been part of their technical training. That kind of expertise lay in a burgeoning field called tissue culture. Salk's proposed vaccine trial would require 10,000 glass tubes of HeLa cells every week from Tuskegee. William F. Scherer, a young postdoctoral researcher at the University of Minnesota, who did early work on the poliovirus using HeLa cells, had instructed students on this topic. He agreed to provide Brown and Henderson the skills they needed. So on January 16, 1953, Brown and Henderson boarded a train in Alabama. And on January 18, 1953, they arrived in the frigid cold of Minnesota on their new mission.

In the 1950s, the Twin Cities of Minneapolis and Saint Paul, Minn., were segregated. Finding campus housing for these two Black men in 1953 was not effortless, particularly because the university's dorms were still new to allowing Black occupants. Rooms were made available near the edge of campus, making the walk to their lab in the brutal weather quite unpleasant. These two Black scientists found their Midwestern hosts to be hospitable, however. Under the Minnesota stars, Brown and Henderson learned the basics of cell and tissue culture and designed their Tuskegee laboratory, preparing for the renovations that would begin when they returned. They needed to be quick studies: Brown stayed in Minnesota for four weeks and Henderson stayed for two. Both were back in Alabama by February 1953.

In April 1953 Scherer headed south to Tuskegee to see the new facility and deliver a precious package. His parcel held contents that were sensitive to temperature swings, and April was one of the few times when Minnesota and Alabama had matching climates. While others on Scherer's airplane drank cocktails (stopping as they flew over dry states), his mind was also on a bottle–the bottle in his carry-on bag. It contained approximately 30 million HeLa cells. When he arrived at the Tuskegee Institute, a liquid was added to those cells, which then fed 40 other bottles. After four days of incubation, each of these bottles contained 30 million more cells, marking the birth of the HeLa cell factory at the Tuskegee Institute.

Inside the Tuskegee HeLa cell factory, cells were grown in a long line of incubators, measured into glass tubes, packaged and then shipped by air to about two dozen medical laboratories all over the country. Tuskegee's mission was difficult for any school, particularly for a small, underfunded one located in the hot South. HeLa cells died when temperatures broiled around 105 degrees Fahrenheit. While air-conditioning had made the Sunbelt bearable and led to a migration to the South in the 1920s, these sensitive cells were doomed if they traveled in hot cars, waited on hot tarmacs or sat in hot airplane cargo hulls. So the leadership of the NFIP asked Maria Telkes, a physical chemist at New York University, to come up with a packaging solution to keep the cells cool while in transit. Telkes, an expert on thermal insulation, calculated and designed a special shipping container that resembled a Russian doll. In it, a box covered with insulation sat inside of another box. The inner box contained a can full of the chemical sodium sulfate decahydrate, which rested on top of the glass tubes and kept the cells from overheating. Once placed in these boxes, the cells had to arrive at their destination within 96 hours. One person drove to airports in Montgomery, Ala., and Columbus, Ga., to make sure that these packages did not miss their flights.

There were many failures in getting the HeLa process right and calls and letters from NFIP officials berated Brown about contaminated samples, low cell output and the arrival of dead cells. Brown, too, was troubled. "The picture at present is distinctly unfavorable," he wrote to the leaders of the NFIP in December 1953. But Norma Gaillard, the cell culture supervisor at Tuskegee, kept making improvements and devised an effective procedure that her technicians followed precisely.

The team vigorously hunted down the sources of contamination and installed special air conditioners to keep the lab cool and remove the last vestige of dust and humidity. With time and effort, the technicians eventually exceeded the 10,000 glass tubes of HeLa cells needed to be shipped in a week. By early 1954 the HeLa cell factory was ready to be part of the world's biggest experiment. It was a good thing, too, because summer–and polio season–was coming.

On April 26, 1954, the field trial for Salk's polio vaccine began. This trial was a medical logistics effort on a scale never seen before. The NFIP employed several drug companies to manufacture the vaccine and also mobilized armies of 20,000 doctors, 40,000 nurses, 1,000 public health professionals, 14,000 school principals, 50,000 teachers and 200,000 volunteers to administer the injections. Overall, nearly 420,000 children were inoculated, and 200,000 were given placebo injections, with an additional 1.2 million other children observed in the study.

Within this huge health campaign was an astronomical number of HeLa cells, which resided inside the 400,000 glass tubes dispatched from a quiet corner of the South. These cells, originating from a Black woman and cultivated by Black scientists, made visible the effectiveness of a long-awaited protection against polio. Ultimately, Thomas Francis, Jr., director of the Poliomyelitis Vaccine Evaluation Center at the University of Michigan, announced on April 12, 1955, that the vaccine was "safe, effective and potent."

The inoculation was approved for distribution, cases of the disease began to drop, and Salk went on to become a national hero. But the role of the Tuskegee Institute and its researchers remained hidden long after the fear of polio faded from the nation's memory.

About the Author

Ainissa Ramirez is a materials scientist and the author of The Alchemy of Us *(MIT Press, 2020). Ramirez writes about little-known contributors to science and has a forthcoming series of children's books about Black inventors (with MIT Kids Press/Candlewick Press). For more of her work, visit www.ainissaramirez.com and follow her on Twitter: @ainissaramirez.*

AIDS in 1988

By Robert C. Gallo and Luc Montagnier

As recently as a decade ago it was widely believed that infectious disease was no longer much of a threat in the developed world. The remaining challenges to public health there, it was thought, stemmed from noninfectious conditions such as cancer, heart disease and degenerative diseases. That confidence was shattered in the early 1980's by the advent of AIDS. Here was a devastating disease caused by a class of infectious agents–retroviruses–that had first been found in human beings only a few years before. In spite of the startling nature of the epidemic, science responded quickly. In the two years from mid-1982 to mid-1984 the outlines of the epidemic were clarified, a new virus–the human immunodeficiency virus (HIV)–was isolated and shown to cause the disease, a blood test was formulated and the virus's targets in the body were established.

Following that initial burst, progress has been steady, albeit slower. Yet in some respects the virus has outpaced science. No cure or vaccine is yet available, and the epidemic continues to spread; disease-causing retroviruses will be among the human population for a long time. In view of that prospect, it is essential to ask where we stand in relation to AIDS in 1988. How was HIV discovered and linked to AIDS? How does the virus cause its devastation? What are the chances that AIDS will spread rapidly outside the known high-risk groups? What are the prospects for a vaccine? For therapy? How can the epidemic most effectively be fought? Those are some of the questions this article and this issue of *Scientific American* have set out to answer.

Like other viruses, retroviruses cannot replicate without taking over the biosynthetic apparatus of a cell and exploiting it for their own ends. What is unique about retroviruses is their capacity to reverse the ordinary flow of genetic information–from DNA to RNA to proteins (which are the cell's structural and functional molecules). The genetic material of a retrovirus is RNA. In addition, the retrovirus carries an enzyme called reverse transcriptase, which can use the viral RNA as a template for making DNA. The viral DNA can integrate itself into the genome (the complement of genetic information) of the host. Having made itself at home among the host's genes, the viral DNA remains latent until it is activated to make new virus particles. The latent DNA can also initiate the process that leads to tumor formation.

Retroviruses and their cancer-causing potential are not new to science. At the beginning of this century several investigators identified transmissible agents in animals that were capable of causing leukemias (cancers of blood cells) as well as solid-tissue tumors. In the succeeding decades retroviruses were identified in many animal species. Yet the life cycle of retroviruses remained obscure until 1970, when Howard M. Temin of the University of Wisconsin at Madison and (independently) David Baltimore of the Massachusetts Institute of Technology discovered reverse transcriptase, confirming Temin's hypothesis that the retroviral life cycle includes an intermediate DNA form, which Temin had called the provirus. The details of viral replication quickly fell into place.

In spite of such discoveries, by the mid-1970's no infectious retroviruses had been found in human beings, and many investigators firmly believed no human retrovirus would ever be found. Their skepticism had several grounds. Many excellent scientists had tried and failed to find such a virus. Moreover, most animal retroviruses had been fairly easy to find, because they replicated in large quantities, and the new virus particles were readily observed in the electron microscope; no such phenomenon had been found in human beings. In spite of this skepticism, by 1980 a prolonged team effort led by one of us (Gallo) paid off in the isolation of the first human retrovirus: human T-lymphotropic virus type I (HTLV-I).

HTLV-I infects T lymphocytes, white blood cells that have a central role in the immune response. The virus causes a rare, highly malignant cancer called adult T-cell leukemia (ATL) that is endemic in parts of Japan, Africa and the Caribbean but is spreading to other regions as well. Two years after the discovery of HTLV-I the same group isolated its close relative, HTLV-II. HTLV-II probably causes some cases of a disease called hairy-cell leukemia as well as T-cell leukemias and lymphomas of a more chronic type than those linked to HTLV-I. The two viruses, however, share some crucial features. They are spread by blood, by sexual intercourse and from mother to child. Both cause disease after a long latency, and both infect T lymphocytes. When AIDS was first recognized, these properties took on great additional significance.

The first AIDS cases were diagnosed in 1981 among young homosexual men in the U.S. Although the syndrome was puzzling, it soon became clear that all its victims suffered from a depletion of a specific subset of T cells–T4 cells–and that as a result they fell prey to pathogens that would easily be controlled by a healthy immune system. A variety of hypotheses were advanced to explain AIDS, including breakdown of the victims' immune systems following repeated exposure to foreign proteins or even to sperm during homosexual intercourse. It seemed more plausible, however, to explain a new syndrome by the appearance of a new infectious agent.

To one of us (Gallo) the likeliest agent was a retrovirus. It had already been shown that the AIDS pathogen, like HTLV-I, could be transmitted by sexual intercourse and by blood. Furthermore, Max Essex of the Harvard School of Public Health had shown that a retrovirus of cats called feline leukemia virus (FeLV) could cause either cancer or immune suppression. Since in most species the infectious retroviruses are closely related, it seemed plausible that the same was true in human beings. Hence the initial hypothesis was that the cause of AIDS was a close relative of HTLV-I. That hypothesis, as it turned out, was wrong. Nonetheless, it was fruitful because it stimulated the search that led to the correct solution.

The retrovirus hypothesis for the origin of AIDS reached the other one of us in France in the following way. Almost as soon as AIDS was first diagnosed, a working group on the syndrome had been formed by a circle of young clinicians and researchers in France. One member of the group, Jacques Leibowitch of the Raymond Poincare Hospital in Paris, had had some contact with Gallo's team and carried the HTLV hypothesis back to France. The members of the French group wanted to test that hypothesis. and they had the biological materials to do so because the group included clinicians with patients afflicted by AIDS or pre-AIDS. What they lacked, however, was the collaboration of virologists experienced in work with retroviruses.

The French author of this article and his colleagues Francoise Barre-Sinoussi and Jean-Claude Chermann at the Pasteur Institute fitted that description. They were engaged in several lines of work on cancer and interferon including attempts to find retroviruses in patients with cancer particularly in cultures of lymphocytes. A member of the working group, Willy Rozenbaum of the Salpetriere Hospital, asked whether they were interested in analyzing tissues from a patient with lymphadenopathy, or swollen glands. (Lymphadenopathy can be an early sign of the process that culminates in AIDS. Such a patient was chosen because finding a virus early in the disease seemed more meaningful than finding one later, when AIDS patients were infected with many opportunistic agents.) The answer was yes, and in January, 1983, a specimen from the swollen lymph node of a young homosexual arrived at Montagnier's laboratory.

The specimen was minced, put into tissue culture and analyzed for reverse transcriptase. After two weeks of culture, reverse-transcriptase activity was detected in the culture medium. A retrovirus was present. But which one? The first possibility that had to be tested was whether the virus was one of the known HTLVs, or perhaps a close relative of them. That possibility was tested using specific HTLV-I reagents supplied by Gallo. The virus did not react significantly with the HTLV-I reagents; a similar result was later obtained with HTLV-II reagents. A strenuous effort was begun to characterize the new agent.

Among the first results of that effort was the finding that the new virus (which was named lymphadenopathy associated virus, or LAV) grew in T4 cells but not in related cells called T8; that finding was made by David Klatzmann and Jean-Claude Gluckman of the Salpetriere Hospital in collaboration with the Pasteur group. It was shown that the virus could kill T4 cells or inhibit their growth. Electron micrographs of the new virus were different from those of HTLV-I and resembled those of a retrovirus of horses. A viral protein called P25 (or P24) that is not present in HTLV-I was identified. In collaboration with virologists from the Claude Bernard Hospital a blood test for lAV antibodies was formulated. Several examples of lAV or lAV-like viruses were isolated from homosexual men, hemophiliacs and central Africans. Early results of applying the blood test were suggestive but not fully conclusive. lAV antibodies were found in a large fraction of lymphadenopathy patients but in only a minority of AIDS patients. Yet the proportion increased as the sensitivity of the test improved. By October, 1983, it had reached 40 percent. At that point one of us (Montagnier) was convinced lAV was the best candidate for the cause of AIDS.

To the other one of us the evidence did not seem so clear. For one thing, results had been obtained (by Gallo and Essex) indicating that some AIDS patients are infected with HTLV-I or a variant of that virus. It is now known that those results stemmed partly from the fact that among people infected with HIV are some who are also infected with the HTLV's. Moreover, only a minority–albeit a substantial one–of AIDS patients had shown serological evidence of lAV infection. In addition, when it was first isolated, lAV could not be grown in large amounts in continuous cell lines. Without large quantities of virus it was difficult to prepare specific lAV reagents that could be used to show that all people with AIDS or pre-AIDS were infected by the same type of virus.

Therefore on the American side much effort was concentrated on growing the pathogen from the blood of AIDS patients in mass, continuous culture. By the end of 1983 that task had been accomplished by the Gallo team: several cell lines had been identified that could support the growth of the new agent. The first reagents for specifically typing this virus were rapidly made. Employing those reagents, it was shown that 48 isolates obtained beginning in early 1983 from AIDS patients and people in risk groups were all the same type of virus, which was called HTLV-III on the American side. A blood test was formulated and used to show that HTLV-III was present in almost all people with AIDS, in a variable proportion of people at risk of the disease (including people who had received blood contaminated by the virus but had no other risk factors) and in no healthy heterosexuals. The cause of AIDS had been conclusively established.

These results confirmed and extended the ones from France. IAV and HTLV-III were soon shown to be the same virus. Before long an international commission had changed its name to HIV, to eliminate confusion caused by two names for the same entity and to acknowledge that the virus does indeed cause AIDS. Thus contributions from our laboratories in roughly equal proportions had demonstrated that the cause of AIDS is a new human retrovirus.

That HIV is the cause of AIDS is by now firmly established. The evidence for causation includes the fact that HIV is a new pathogen, fulfilling the original postulate of "new disease, new agent." In addition, although the original tests found evidence of HIV infection in only a fraction of people with AIDS, newer and more sensitive methods make it possible to find such evidence in almost every individual with AIDS or pre-AIDS. Studies of blood-transfusion recipients indicate that people exposed to HIV who have no other risk factors develop AIDS. The epidemiological evidence shows that in every country studied so far AIDS has appeared only after HIV. What is more, HIV infects and kills the very T4 cells that are depleted in AIDS. Although the causative role of HIV in AIDS has been questioned, to us it seems clear that the cause of AIDS is as well established as that of any other human disease.

Soon after the causation was established, a series of findings began to fill in the scientific picture of HIV. In a remarkably short time the genetic material of the virus was cloned and sequenced (in our laboratories and several others). The genetic complexity of HIV began to emerge when a gene called TAT was discovered by William A Haseltine of the Dana-Farber Cancer Institute, Flossie Wong-Staal of the National Cancer Institute and their collaborators. Such complexity is significant because it underlies the capacity of HIV to remain latent for a long period, then undergo a burst of replication, a pattern that may hold the key to the pathology of AIDS.

There were other significant early findings. One of us (Gallo), with his colleagues Mikulas Popovic and Suzanne Gartner, showed that HIV could infect not only the T4 cell but also another type of white blood cell, the macrophage. The same one of us, working with his colleagues Beatrice H. Hahn, George M. Shaw and Wong-Staal, found HIV in brain tissues. It seems possible that the macrophage, which can cross the blood-brain barrier, may bring virus into the brain, explaining the central-nervous-system pathology seen in many AIDS patients.

How the virus infects both T4 cells and macrophages became clear when Robin A. Weiss of the Chester Beatty Laboratories and, independently, Klatzmann and the Pasteur group showed that HIV enters its target cells by interacting with the molecule called CD4. CD4 has a significant role in the immune function of T4 lymphocytes and also serves as a marker for that group of cells. The early work by the British and French teams showed that HIV infects cells by binding to CD4. Hence only cells bearing that marker can be infected. (Although CD4 is the marker for the T4 cells, it is also found in smaller numbers on some macrophages, allowing them to be infected.)

Several additional findings rounded out the early discoveries. The potential of the epidemic to spread beyond the original risk groups was shown when Robert R. Redfield and one of us (Gallo) demonstrated that HIV can be transmitted during heterosexual intercourse. Members of the Gallo team also showed that the genetic makeup of the virus is highly variable from strain to strain, a fact that may complicate the attempt to formulate an AIDS vaccine.

After the rapid initial advance the pace slowed somewhat and began to approximate that of a more mature area of research. Yet the continuing work was not without surprises. In October 1985, one of us (Montagnier) was engaged in analyzing blood samples brought to his laboratory by a visiting investigator from Portugal. Many of the samples were from people who had lived in Guinea-Bissau, a former Portuguese colony in West Africa. Among them were some people who had been diagnosed by Portuguese clinicians and investigators as having AIDS in spite of the fact that their blood showed no sign of HIV infection.

One sample, in fact, was negative for HIV using the most sophisticated techniques available at the time. Yet workers in the laboratory were able to isolate a virus from the patient's blood. DNA "probes" (short pieces of DNA from the HIV genome) were then prepared. If the new virus were closely related to the original AIDS agent, those probes would bind to its genetic material. As it turned out, there was little binding, and it became clear that the new isolate was not simply a strain of the original AIDS virus but a new virus designated HIV-2. Soon a second example was isolated by workers at the Claude Bernard Hospital; many others followed.

In evolutionary terms HIV-2 is clearly related to HIV-1, the virus responsible for the main AIDS epidemic. The two viruses are similar in their overall structure and both can cause AIDS, although the pathogenic potential of HIV-2 is not as well established as that of the first AIDS virus. HIV-2 is found mainly in West Africa, whereas HIV-1 is concentrated in central Africa and other regions of the world. The finding of HIV-2 suggests that other undiscovered HIVs may exist, filling out a spectrum of related pathogens.

The isolation of HIV-2 immediately raises the question of the evolutionary origins of these viruses. Although the answer to that question has not been found, some hints have been provided by the discovery in other primate species of related viruses called simian immunodeficiency viruses (SN's). The first such virus, found in the macaque monkey, is designated SN macaque. Isolated and characterized by Ronald C. Desrosiers and his co-workers at the New England Regional Primate Research Center in collaboration with Essex and his colleague Phyllis Kanki, SN macaque has been shown to be closely related to HIV-2, raising the possibility that HIV-2 may have come into human beings relatively recently from another primate species.

No such close simian relative has been found for HIV-1 (although the right group of primates may not yet have been studied in sufficient detail). Hence the origin of HIV-1 remains more mysterious than the origin of its relative HIV-2. It is likely, however, that HIV-1 has been in human beings for some time. One of us (Gallo), with Temin, has used the divergence among HIV strains and the virus's probable rate of mutation to estimate how long the virus has infected people. It was tentatively concluded that HIV has infected human beings for more than 20 years but less than 100, an estimate compatible with those by other workers and with our knowledge of the epidemic.

Where was HIV hiding all those years, and why are we only now experiencing an epidemic? Both of us think the answer is that the virus has been present in small, isolated groups in central Africa or elsewhere for many years. In such groups the spread of HIV might have been quite limited and the groups themselves may have had little contact with the outside world. As a result the virus could have been contained for decades.

That pattern may have been altered when the way of life in central Africa began to change. People migrating from remote areas to urban centers no doubt brought HIV with them. Sexual mores in the city were different from what they had been in the village, and blood transfusions were commoner. Consequently HIV may have spread freely. Once a pool of infected people had been established, transport networks and the generalized exchange of blood products would have carried it to every corner of the world. What had been remote and rare became global and common.

What weapons are available against this scourge? Perhaps the best weapon is knowledge. One key form of knowledge is a deeper understanding of HIV, its life cycle and the mechanisms by which it causes disease. Although HIV kills T4 cells directly, it has become clear that the direct killing of those cells is not sufficient to explain the depletion seen in AIDS. Indirect mechanisms must also be at work. What are they?

Many possibilities have been suggested. Infection by HIV can cause infected and uninfected cells to fuse into giant cells called syncytia, which are not functional. Autoimmune responses, in which the immune system attacks the body's own tissues, may also be at work. What is more, HIV infected cells may send out protein signals that weaken or destroy other cells of the immune system. In addition HIV is fragile, and as the virus particle leaves its host cell, a molecule called gp120 frequently falls off the virus's outer coat. As Dani P. Bolognesi of the Duke University Medical Center and his co-workers have shown, gp120 can bind to the CD4 molecules of uninfected cells. When that complex is recognized by the immune system, cells thus marked may be destroyed.

That list does not exhaust the possibilities. One of us (Montagnier) is exploring the possibility that the binding of the virus to its target cells triggers the release of enzymes called proteases. Proteases digest proteins, and if they were released in abnormal quantities, they might weaken white blood cells and shorten their lives. The various proposed mechanisms are not exclusive, and several may operate at once. Yet one is probably central, and some of the most significant work on AIDS is that of distinguishing the central mechanism from the peripheral ones that accompany it.

Although it is clear that a large enough dose of the right strain of HIV can cause AIDS on its own, cofactors can clearly influence the progression of the disease. People whose immune systems are weakened before HIV infection may progress toward AIDS more quickly than others; stimulation of the immune system in response to later infections may also hasten disease progression.

Interaction with other pathogens may also increase the likelihood that AIDS will develop. Specifically, a herpes virus called human B-cell lymphotropic virus (HBLV) or human herpes virus 6 (HHV-6) that was discovered in the laboratory of one of us (Gallo) can interact with HIV in a way that may increase the severity of HIV infection. Ordinarily HHV-6 is easily controlled by the immune system. In a person whose immune system is impaired by HIV, however, HHV-6 may replicate more freely, becoming a threat to health. In addition, although one of the main hosts of HHV-6 is a white blood cell called the B cell, the virus can also infect T4 lymphocytes. If the T cell is simultaneously infected by HIV, HHV-6 can activate the latent AIDS virus, further impairing the immune system and worsening the cycle.

Clearly, in spite of rapid progress there are many gaps in our understanding of HIV and AIDS. Should we panic? The answer is no, for several reasons. The most obvious is that panic does no good. The second reason is that it now seems unlikely HIV infection will spread as rapidly outside the original high-risk groups in the industrial countries as it has within them. A third reason is that this disease is not beyond the curative power of science. Although current knowledge is imperfect, it is sufficient to provide confidence that effective therapies and a vaccine will be developed.

The possibilities for therapy are particularly impressive. In the first phase of the search for AIDS therapies it was necessary to exploit any drug that seemed to provide even a remote chance of combating HIV infection. A variety of compounds formulated for other purposes were taken off the shelf and tested. Most were of little value, but one (AZT), originally formulated as an anticancer drug, turned out to be the first effective anti-AIDS agent. More recently, an experimental regimen in which AZT is alternated with the related compound known as dideoxycytidine offers even greater promise.

Bringing AZT into clinical use was a significant accomplishment, because it gave hope that AIDS would not remain incurable forever. As a form of therapy, however, AZT is not perfect and will probably be supplanted by less toxic agents formulated on the basis of what is known about the HIV life cycle. One promising agent is CD4, the molecule that serves as the viral receptor. Early tests show that soluble CD4 can bind to the virus and prevent it from infecting new cells. Many other drugs are in trials; one of them, perhaps combined with compounds that bolster the immune system, may provide therapy for HIV infection.

In assessing the progress that has been made toward achieving fully effective AIDS therapy, it must be kept in mind that this work has two facets. In addition to combating a complex and evasive pathogen, it must pioneer entirely new areas of medicine. The reason is that there are few effective treatments for viral diseases-and almost none for retroviruses. There are various reasons for this, among them the fact that viruses (unlike bacteria, for which effective therapies exist) always appropriate the biosynthetic apparatus of the host cell. As a result drugs effective against viruses tend to damage mammalian cells. Yet we are confident that the dual goals of pioneering science and clinical effectiveness will be met.

What is true of therapy is also true of vaccines: an AIDS vaccine will be a pioneering scientific achievement. Since the HIV genome has the capacity to integrate into the chromosomes of the host cell, little serious consideration has been given to using preparations containing the whole virus as a vaccine. An AIDS vaccine must consist of subunits, or parts, of the virus in the right combination. Yet experience with subunit vaccines is slight. Indeed, so far only a few subunit vaccines have proved practical. Much work is underway to find the combination of HIV subunits that will yield the greatest protective response. As in the case of therapy, we believe there will be a practical vaccine against HIV.

Perhaps an even more persuasive reason for hope is that even without a vaccine or a cure, what is already known could bring the epidemic under control. The blood supply has already been largely secured by the presence of a blood test. Moreover, the modes of transmission of HIV–blood, sexual intercourse and from mother to child–are firmly established. Hence any individual can drastically reduce his or her risk of infection. If such knowledge were applied everywhere, there would be a sharp leveling off in the spread of HIV infection, as there has been in some groups in the developed world. The lesson here is that there is a need for education about HIV infection–in clear, explicit language and as early as possible.

Yet there are parts of the epidemic where education alone is not sufficient, and it is in those areas that humanity will be tested. Users of intravenous drugs, for example, are notoriously resistant to educational campaigns alone. It seems clear that the effort to control AIDS must be aimed in part at eradicating the conditions that give rise to drug addiction. Those conditions are in turn linked to social and economic patterns. Eliminating the disease may entail eliminating some of the social differentials that form the substratum of drug abuse.

It is also the case that in some areas of the developing world, education alone will not stem the epidemic. Education is necessary, but it must be accompanied by other measures. In central Africa–the part of the world most beleaguered by AIDs–there are few facilities for blood testing and few technicians trained to perform tests. Furthermore, the blood tests used in the U.S. and Western Europe are too expensive to be helpful. As a result the virus is still being spread by contaminated blood, long after that form of transmission has been practically eliminated in the industrial countries.

To help change this situation, the World AIDS Foundation has made improving the situation in central Africa its highest priority. The foundation (along with its parent, the Franco-American AIDS Foundation) was formed as part of the agreement that resolved a lawsuit between France and the U.S. over the AIDS blood test. The parent foundation receives 80 percent of the royalties from the French and American blood tests; the World AIDS Foundation in turn receives 25 percent of that. Much thought has been given to how to allocate the funds, and the first project (carried out in conjunction with the World Health Organization) will be realized in several African countries. It will include training technicians to perform blood tests, establishing one HIV-free blood center and increasing public education about HIV transmission.

Efforts such as this one, coupling public and private funds and energies, will be essential to stopping AIDS. As we stated above, both of us are certain that science will ultimately find a cure and a vaccine for AIDS. But not tomorrow. The AIDS virus (and other human retroviruses) will be with us for a long time. During that time no intelligent person can expect the necessary solutions to come solely from authorities such as scientists, governments or corporations. All of us must accept responsibilities: to learn how HIV is spread, to reduce risky behavior, to raise our voices against acceptance of the drug culture and to avoid stigmatizing victims of the disease. If we can accept such responsibilities, the worst element of nightmare will have been removed from the AIDS epidemic.

Cures for Sickle Cell Disease Arrive After a Painful Journey

By Maryn McKenna

Nathan Wood is 15, lanky and tall. He longs to play basketball; he lives in Yonkers, just outside New York City, and his high school and city parks provide plenty of opportunity for shooting hoops. But his body won't allow it. Nathan was born with sickle cell disease, an inherited condition that makes round red blood cells collapse into sticky crescents. The distorted cells clump inside blood vessels, depriving tissues of oxygen and inflicting excruciating pain. Exercise or stress or even just changes in routine can trigger a crisis, so Nathan's mother, Melissa Wood, has often homeschooled him and drives him everywhere–a rare thing in New York, where kids prize their independence.

But the caution is necessary because Nathan's sickle crises are so frequent. About twice a month, he estimates, he feels the first throbs in his hands or joints, signaling the approach of pain so intense that it forces him to lie flat in bed until it passes. And about twice a year the crises get bad enough to put him into Children's Hospital at Montefiore in the Bronx, where he's been a patient since he was a baby.

He would very much like his life to change. "Just get back into basketball, start going to school, and doing what I want to do as a kid," he said in a chat at Montefiore on a sunny June day when his family had brought him in for blood tests. "And not be separated from other people and not be different."

Nathan might soon have that chance. For the first time in the 114 years since sickle cell was originally described in a medical journal–although it existed, undefined, for millennia before then–therapies may end a disease that afflicts 100,000 Americans and millions more throughout the world. Last December the U.S. Food and Drug Administration approved two gene-editing treatments that compensate for the mutated DNA that causes sickling. In clinical trials, most patients who received the treatments had no pain episodes afterward, an indication their cells had ceased to sickle. In the wake of that success, several other gene therapies are moving through clinical trials, and Nathan is joining one.

Once he begins treatment this January in Nashville, Tenn., Nathan will face a grueling year of multiple procedures, including months of isolation in a hospital. But if the treatment succeeds, it will remake his life–and his family's. For Melissa, her fiancé and Nathan's two siblings, his illness has been a constant worry. "I got the call a few days after he was born," Melissa says. "I'm looking at this perfectly healthy child, and it just took all my happiness away in that instant. And from there I've had him in a bubble. So this will kind of ease me off of him a bit."

The approved new therapies and the ones likely to come after them hold the potential to alter the entire experience of sickle cell–and, some advocates hope, to change the way medicine treats people with many other conditions. Sickle cell history includes triumphant breakthroughs in science: Research on the illness signaled the dawn of the era of molecular medicine. Progress in testing and treatment involved dogged work by physicians who would not give up on their patients. Disseminating awareness of risk required ferocious activism by communities. Yet for more than 100 years medical research and practice have also illustrated the costs of racial disregard and a lack of commitment to disadvantaged communities. At the start of the second century of sickle cell science, all those factors will determine what the future of medicine may be.

At its simplest, sickle cell disease is a problem caused by the smallest unit in genetics: a change in a single nucleotide–one of about three billion in the human genome–within a gene that directs the production of one part of hemoglobin, the protein that carries oxygen molecules through the blood. Hundreds of millions of hemoglobin molecules are packed into each red blood cell. The hemoglobin produced by the genetic variant can change shape as it gives up the oxygen it is transporting. That shift forces the enclosing cell to deform and turn rigid, taking on the sickled appearance that gives the disease its name. The distorted cells lodge in blood vessels instead of slipping smoothly through them as round red blood cells do.

The nucleotide substitution in the HBB gene–producing what's known as hemoglobin S, in contrast to normal hemoglobin A–is heritable. Someone who receives one altered gene from one parent is at risk of sickle cell trait, a condition in which few red blood cells are affected. Someone who receives two copies of the gene–a one-in-four chance if both parents carry it–will have the disease. That leaves them at risk for pain crises, anemia as the stiffened cells break down, organ damage because sickled cells carry less oxygen to tissues, a dangerous blockage of blood vessels in the lungs called acute chest syndrome, high blood pressure, and stroke.

Researchers working in western Africa have traced accounts of sickle cell crises back hundreds of years, noting that the symptoms had specific names in different languages and were understood to occur in generations of families. Sickled cells have been identified in modern studies of mummified tissue from Egypt dating to 3200 B.C.E. and skeletons from Kuwait that were buried in about 200 B.C.E. Scientists at the National Human Genome Research Institute, part of the National Institutes of Health, used a family-tree analysis of almost 3,000 genomes to estimate that the sickle cell mutation first arose in the Sahara approximately 7,300 years ago and was subsequently carried through the African continent by migrations.

At the time that mutation appeared, the Sahara was not a desert; it was green and wet, containing grasslands and forests and permanent lakes, along with the animal and insect life suited to those ecosystems. A type of malaria parasite has been identified in fossils that date back at least 20 million years, and the disease has been infecting humanity from our first emergence. And that seems to be a reason the mutation spread: A single copy of the gene–effectively, having sickle cell trait–conferred protection against severe malaria. It would have been a formidable advantage for people living in some of the most malarious places on the planet. This dynamic offers an explanation for why the sickle cell mutation persisted in sub-Saharan

Africa, which still has the highest prevalence of sickle cell disease, and spread around the Mediterranean and into the Middle East.

Different strains of malaria arrived in South America, the Caribbean and the U.S. South in the 1600s. The disease devastated indentured European laborers and enslaved Native Americans. The observation that some African people–kidnapped and then enslaved in the New World–were protected from the worst effects of malaria was perceived as extra incentive for their captivity. Apologists for slavery argued it proved that Africans were intended by nature to be agricultural laborers. Economist Elena Esposito of the University of Lausanne in Switzerland has shown, using sale records incorporating places of origin, that planters paid a premium for enslaved Africans whom they assumed possessed resistance to the disease.

Although there have been many waves of migration from Africa and the Mediterranean to the U.S., historians say much of the sickle cell disease in people of African heritage in the Americas may be traced to the enslavement and transport of their ancestors. The link between sickle cell and a forcibly disadvantaged group set the pattern for how U.S. society would respond to the disease.

The modern study of sickle cell disease began with a descendant of that African diaspora after an unusual set of circumstances allowed him to bypass medicine's racial segregation. During the 1904 Christmas holidays a dental student in Chicago named Walter Clement Noel sought help for what felt like pneumonia. Noel was Black, but he was not a member of the post–Civil War Great Migration into northern cities. He was a member of an affluent family on the Caribbean island of Grenada and was studying at the Chicago College of Dental Surgery. Benefits available through that post made medical care affordable at four downtown hospitals that Noel otherwise would have been unlikely to approach for care. He crossed the street from his lodgings to what is now Rush University Medical Center and was treated by faculty physician James Herrick and his intern, Ernest Irons.

The two men did a thorough exam of Noel, noting a cough, fever, swollen lymph nodes, a slight heart murmur, and scars on his legs from recurrent ulcers. Nothing notable showed up in a urinalysis, but Irons noticed something odd about Noel's red blood cells under a microscope. When Herrick described Noel's case in a medical journal in 1910, he wrote that the blood contained "a large number of thin, elongated, sickle-shaped and crescent-shaped forms."

Noel stayed in the hospital for a month, receiving nourishing food and iron supplements but never a diagnosis. "We were at a loss to account for this peculiar complexus of symptoms," Herrick admitted in his write-up. The two doctors saw him a number of times until he graduated from dental school in 1907, and then they lost track of him. (They might never have known that he died in Grenada in 1916, ostensibly from pneumonia but probably from complications of sickle cell.) Three other patients with the same symptoms were reported in the next 12 years, in Virginia, Maryland and Missouri. But in 1923 physicians began to recognize the disease in dozens of people. In 1924 American medicine agreed that the constellation of disordered cells, symptoms and family history represented a unique disease rather than the effects of any known pathogen.

There would, of course, have been many more patients than those–but during this period the medical workforce most would have consulted was being eliminated. In 1910, the same year Herrick published his report on Noel, a so-called reform plan for U.S. medical education forced the closure of all but two historically Black medical schools, almost wiping out training for Black physicians because medical schools were otherwise largely segregated. That pushed Black people's participation in the medical workforce far below their representation in the population. The imbalance has persisted: in 2022 fewer than 6 percent of physicians in the U.S. identified as Black, although more than 13 percent of the population chose that identity in 2020 census data. Researchers say those closed schools would have trained several generations of Black physicians and mentors, an estimated 35,000 missing from the field.

"At the same time that you have this new disease being described, the workforce to take care of [patients] plummets," says James Taylor VI, director of the Center for Sickle Cell Disease at Howard University. The center at this prominent historically Black university is the oldest one in the U.S. The limits on Black people working as physicians and in other health-care roles, he says, are "the root of so many of the disparities we still see today."

Restricting Black participation in the medical profession deprived sickle cell patients of health-care workers who would have best understood their needs and may have contributed to the maligning of people experiencing sickling crises as addicts faking pain to obtain opioids. It also might have enabled an enduring pattern in sickle cell research: biochemical discovery racing far ahead of improved patient care.

Chemist Linus Pauling, later a two-time winner of the Nobel Prize, identified the hemoglobin defect in 1949. Once he identified the cause of sickle cell as a mutant hemoglobin molecule, Pauling dubbed sickle cell anemia a "molecular disease." That framing effectively launched the biomedical era of newly powerful laboratory research. Mark T. Gladwin, a longtime sickle cell researcher who is dean of the University of Maryland School of Medicine, says "sickle cell disease has always led the cutting edge of science discovery, whether it's understanding the regulation of [genetic] promoter sequences or understanding protein biochemistry and folding. The concepts behind prion disease and amyloidosis, protein-folding diseases, those were predicted by sickle polymerization."

One of the first drugs to meaningfully help patients was not a novel antisickling agent. Instead it was penicillin, which became available in U.S. pharmacies in 1945. Sickling makes children more vulnerable to a variety of infections, but when child mortality was already high, deaths associated with sickle cell did not stand out from other childhood illness. Antibiotics made it possible to cure those infections, and by preventing death, they allowed the disease to be perceived in survivors. (Twice-daily doses of antibiotics are still routinely prescribed for children younger than five years who have sickle cell disease.)

The first drug that actually made an impact on the disease process of sickle cell was a compound called hydroxyurea. It was originally a cancer drug, but researchers showed it could also prompt production of a type of hemoglobin that is present before birth and in infants but fades after a few months of life. Cells with this kind of hemoglobin resist sickling–an explanation for why newborns with the illness do not experience sickle crises. Hydroxyurea reduces sickle crises and hospitalization by half. Yet it was not tested against the disease or approved by the FDA until the 1990s, nearly 50 years after Pauling's discovery of the sickle cell mutation.

The dearth of treatments created a kind of feedback loop. Sickle cell looked like a disease in which no progress could be made; because of that, new researchers were discouraged from entering the field, which delayed progress further. Vivien Sheehan, a hematologist and associate professor of pediatrics at Emory University School of Medicine, who leads a lab studying the genomics of sickle cell, recalls an esteemed faculty member telling her during her training not to pursue sickle cell as a career. "I can picture what he thought," she says. "We had one old drug; there was no pharma interest, no gene therapy. NIH funding was low compared with other genetic diseases."

What changed the picture was activism. In 1970 a physician named Robert B. Scott, Jr., was a faculty member at what was then a predominantly white medical institution that later became part of Virginia Commonwealth University. That year he wrote a blistering editorial in the Journal of the American Medical Association. He laid out how little funding sickle cell was receiving either from the government or from private donors compared with other genetic diseases. As an example, he estimated that research into cystic fibrosis, which occurred in one out of 2,940 children, received 65 NIH grants in 1968; sickle cell, affecting one in 500 children, received 22. And, highlighting the lack of generational wealth in the Black community, he also estimated that muscular dystrophy research benefited from $7.2 million in volunteer contributions, compared with just $50,000 for sickle cell, which had no national advocacy organization.

Scott did not say explicitly that race was the reason sickle cell had been neglected, but the conclusion was obvious. The following year the Black Panther Party announced it was making sickle cell one of its main priorities, creating a People's Sickle Cell Anemia

Research Foundation and launching a massive educational campaign that included community events offering free screening for sickle cell trait and disease. To put both the editorial and the campaign into context: The Civil Rights Act had passed in 1964, and Martin Luther King, Jr., was assassinated in 1968. A national election was looming in 1972. Maybe to heal the nation–or maybe, more cynically, to attract Black votes–President Richard M. Nixon proposed a sickle cell research program. The National Sickle Cell Anemia Control Act passed in 1972, committing the NIH to creating 10 research and training centers around the country. But crucially, the bill allowed no new money for the effort; instead it was funded by other NIH programs' budgets. So within several years sickle cell research was back to depending on the energy of individual researchers.

To be clear, these efforts produced life-saving results. In 1997 researchers established that periodic transfusions could reduce the risk of stroke in children diagnosed with sickle cell. In 2007 researchers in France demonstrated that children with sickle cell could be cured with a bone marrow transplant from a donor who was an exact immunological match, such as a full sibling. In 2009 investigators in the U.S. established that a similar process could cure adults. A burst of innovation in the past decade brought three new drugs into sickle cell care: l-glutamine, approved in 2017, and crizanlizumab and voxelotor, both approved in 2019. But researchers say uptake of these new agents has been slow. And hydroxyurea, still the best drug, faces a major usage hurdle: it is contraindicated for pregnant people, based on animal studies and limited human data showing it can produce birth defects.

Sickle cell experts hope more treatments and cures are coming. "What we currently have approved for drug therapies is not adequate," says hematologist Modupe Idowu, medical director of the UT Physicians Comprehensive Adult Sickle Cell Center in Houston, which treats about 1,300 adults with sickle cell disease. "Hydroxyurea remains the gold standard, but some patients really have reservations about it. Patients must stay on these indefinitely, and they are not curative. And patients continue to have pain episodes, and they continue to have complications."

Until now, the only true cure for sickle cell has been a bone marrow transplant from a family member who is a perfect immunological match. But only a few patients–between 10 and 20 percent–can identify one. The seemingly benign therapy of periodic transfusions carries its own risks, including a toxic overload of iron that has to be scavenged from the body. And over time excruciating sickling crises rewire pain pathways in the body, leaving patients with chronic pain.

The new gene therapies are an extraordinary scientific achievement, but they are difficult to obtain. The two recent treatments, Casgevy and Lyfgenia, became two of the most expensive drugs on the U.S. market when they were approved, costing $2.2 million and $3.1 million, respectively. Those prices cover only the gene editing of a patient's own cells–"not the coverage of the hospital stays, or all their visits with me, or the transfusions they will need in preparation, or the central line they will need placed, or the fertility preservation they may want first," says Kerry Morrone, an assistant professor at Albert Einstein College of Medicine in New York City and director of the sickle cell program treating Nathan at Children's Hospital at Montefiore. (The clinical trial Nathan has entered will pay for his care.) Approval, in other words, may not equal access and may not meaningfully improve the lives of most people with the disease today.

The gene therapies are built on the back of a stem cell transplant. A patient must receive transfusions to force down the number of sickled cells in their bloodstream, then growth factors to make sure they produce enough new stem cells; they need other drugs to move the cells out from their bone marrow. The stem cells are harvested in a procedure resembling an extended blood draw and sent to the drug companies for genetic editing. Once they are returned, the patient undergoes therapy to kill their disordered cells before the edited ones are infused. The entire process can take a year.

The length, complexity and expense can prompt deep uncertainty in people living with sickle cell disease. Melissa Creary is one of them.

She is a social scientist at the University of Michigan School of Public Health who studies the ways science, culture and policy intersect in sickle cell. She is also a sickle cell patient, having been diagnosed at three years old, and for much of her life she experienced few complications. Then, six years ago, when she was 40, an unexpected complication turned her mild case extreme, inflicting severe pain crises and requiring a strict schedule of doctors' appointments every five weeks, as well as a complex medication regimen.

"I do not ever miss one of these appointments," Creary says. "I know what the schedule looks like almost a year in advance. I have my community signed up for who's going to be my buddy because I'm kind of worthless for that day."

She is considering gene therapy. "I'm having conversations with my providers, people I know personally, people I know professionally," she says. Her mother wants to see her cured. Yet Creary's clinician colleagues urged her to wait. Creary cannot be sure what consequences the treatment might have for her career, finances and support network. If an adult treatment program is not set up in Michigan, she would have to be hospitalized in another state.

"I don't want to have sickle cell anymore, either, despite the ways in which it has literally crafted who I am as a person, as a scholar," Creary says. "If I could be untethered to the health-care system through gene therapy, I would jump through 18 hoops. But jumping through those hoops also means all kinds of risks, known and unknown."

Creary advises various groups on equity and antiracism in medicine, and she is also thinking about how the promise and uncertainties of the new therapies will be communicated to other patients. People with sickle cell come into contact with medicine when they are experiencing the worst pain of their lives, she points out; they may act out because of that or have difficulty expressing themselves. They are likely to encounter racism not only in the outside world but within medicine as well, making it challenging to navigate care and to have their concerns taken seriously. And now they may be confronting the possibility that a functional cure could be out of reach for them because of decisions made by insurance companies or by politicians refusing Medicaid expansion plans.

"At the end of the day, this is about trust and mistrust," Creary says. "We haven't done what we need to do in order to build the trust with this population, in order for the science to be as efficacious as it needs to be."

Sickle cell medicine now has two goals. One is to imagine the next genetic therapies, perhaps developing gene edits that can be inserted into a patient without disrupting their immune system and blood cells first. The other, even more important, is to envision fair, thorough and accessible care. Patients and researchers agree that is what's most essential now.

Historian Keith Wailoo, a professor of history and public affairs at Princeton University and author of several books on sickle cell, says there has been an ongoing mismatch between what medicine has prioritized and what patients need. He co-chaired a committee at the National Academies of Sciences, Engineering, and Medicine that, in 2023, published a report on whether equity can be a required part of innovation. "The core question was, Is it possible to have a society where equitable access to innovation is more than just an afterthought?" he says. "The moment that we're in right now should be an object lesson for how we need to innovate in a smarter way."

Across the U.S., medical centers that have transplant programs are evaluating whether they can deliver the new therapies. They also are scrutinizing who might pay for the procedures and associated care because the cost is beyond the reach of most families, and no one knows how insurance companies will respond.

The Centers for Medicare and Medicaid Services are currently negotiating to set prices; after that, state governments would have to opt in. The limitations of medical insurance are not a new story to Americans, but in this case, whether a patient is eligible for these therapies may depend on not just their age and the state of their disease but where they live.

Clinicians and patients did not have discussions about these things in the past, because the concept of transforming the disease was out of reach. But they are having them now. "Before this time, our conversations about disparities have been about making sure patients with sickle cell are getting clinical care," says Seethal A. Jacob, director of the pediatric sickle cell program at Indiana University and Riley Children's Health in Indianapolis, which is applying to offer gene therapy. "But now we need to talk about how we close the gap of disparities in access to these treatments."

Sickle cell medicine has reached a potentially transformative moment. The history of sickle cell is a tale of bravery and agony, effort and neglect, that mirrors the history of the Black experience in America. If these new therapies and the ones that come after them prove truly successful, individual lives will be completely changed. And perhaps a long-standing wound of inequity and injustice might begin to be healed.

About the Author

Maryn McKenna is a journalist specializing in public health, global health and food policy and a contributing editor at Scientific American. She is author of Big Chicken: The Incredible Story of How Antibiotics Created Modern Agriculture and Changed the Way the World Eats *(National Geographic Books, 2017).*

Section 4: The Art of Surgery

4.1 Ambroise Paré
By Sir Geoffrey Keynes

4.2 The Late Joseph Lister: The Father of Antiseptic Surgery
By John B. Huber, A. M. , M. D.

Ambroise Paré

By Sir Geoffrey Keynes

The extent to which an individual can influence the course of history has often been questioned, and it may be that in world affairs it is apt to be exaggerated. But in narrower spheres the importance of individuals is difficult to deny. In the history of surgery it is possible to point to a number of pioneers who shaped events literally with their hands. Outstanding among these is the figure of the 16th-century Frenchman Ambroise Paré. In the century of giants such as Raphael and Titian, Luther and Erasmus, Paracelsus and Vesalius, Paré was equally famous as the foremost surgeon of his time. He was the surgeon of kings and an idol of the common people. He was also one of the founders of civilized surgery–an innovator who introduced many practices which are in common use today.

His career reads rather more like that of a soldier than of a man of medicine. Paré was a military surgeon, a participant in the many wars between the kings of France and the Holy Roman Empire of Charles V, and most of his inventions in surgery were made on the battlefield. But he took care to record his adventures and discoveries in a series of books, and so his work became a part of the history of medicine.

Paré rose from a humbler origin than most of the other great figures of the Renaissance. Born in 1510 in a village of northwestern France, he was the son of a valet and barber. Following the example of an older brother and a brother-in-law, young Ambroise decided to become a barber-surgeon. This was the lowest grade of the medical hierarchy in 16th-century France, but it was the despised barber-surgeons who performed nearly all surgery, for the higher ranks of "surgeons" and physicians thought it degrading to use their hands. Lacking Latin and Greek, Paré could not aspire to admission to the medical profession, that is, election to the Faculty of Physicians of Paris or the Surgeons of the College of St. Côme. He therefore went to work, at the age of 22 or 23, as apprentice to a barber-surgeon in Paris, learning bloodletting, cupping and operations for cataract, hernia and gallstones.

His common sense and remarkable powers of observation soon won him an appointment as resident surgeon at the only public hospital in Paris, the Hôtel-Dieu. After three years he somehow attracted the attention of the Mareschal de Montejan, a colonel general of the army. Although Paré was still only an apprentice, de Montejan made him his staff surgeon. In those days there was no organized army medical service, the only doctors in the field being those attached to the person of a leading officer.

It was de Montejan's luck or foresight to create an opening for a young man who was to become one of the greatest military surgeons of all time. Paré soon realized that the accepted methods of treating the wounded were inhuman and inefficient, and he proceeded to introduce his own improvements.

It was generally believed that gunshot wounds were poisoned or infected by the gunpowder, and doctors customarily cauterized the wounds with "oil of elders scalding hot, with a little treacle mixed therewith." Aside from being extremely painful, the hot oil must have caused the death of tissues, thus helping to bring on the very complications it sought to avoid. Paré at first used the conventional treatment. One day, running out of oil, he substituted an unheated dressing made up of "digestive of the yoke of an egg, oil of roses and turpentine." "That night," he later related, "I was unable to sleep in peace. I thought that for lack of cauterization I would find the wounded poisoned to death, which made me rise in the very early morning to visit them." To his delight, he found the patients in much better shape than those who had been treated with hot oil.

Paré's "digestive mixture" was clearly not antiseptic in the modern sense, but it at least formed a protective layer and led only to a mild formation of pus instead of the acute inflammation which followed the application of scalding oil. It was the beginning of the rational treatment of gunshot wounds. Paré experimented with other dressings and later described his discovery in his first book, *The Method of Curing Wounds Made by Gunshot.*

Paré's successful innovation, together with his humane attitude toward the sufferings of the soldiers, established his reputation as a military surgeon, and his services were in great demand. But when de Montejan died not long afterward, Paré was so overcome with grief at the loss of his commander that he left the army and returned to Paris. He resumed the study of anatomy so that he might at length pass the examination for admission as a qualified barber-surgeon. This he achieved in 1541, at the age of 31. He practiced surgery in Paris, married Jeanne Mazelin, a woman of the people, and acquired some property on the left bank of the Seine and in the country at Meudon.

Yet Paré did not stay settled in Paris. He shortly joined the Vicomte de Rohan in the siege of Perpignan, and for the next 30 years he pursued his career as a military surgeon, taking part in a series of campaigns which brought him ever increasing credit as a surgeon and a reputation for outstanding courage, common sense and honesty. During this time he was surgeon to four successive French kings–Henry II, Francis II, Charles IX and Henry III. Paré's adventures are recorded in a remarkably entertaining and historically valuable autobiography. He wrote it to reply to a jealous physician who had attacked his novel surgical methods; fortunately his enthusiasm so carried him away that the reply became a long account of his experiences, which he titled *Apology and Treatise Containing the Journeys to Diverse Places.*

At Perpignan Paré distinguished himself by removing from the shoulder of the Grand Master of Artillery a bullet which had baffled other surgeons. His method of locating the course of a bullet in the body was to place the limb in the exact position it had occupied at the time the victim was shot. It was during another campaign with the Vicomte de Rohan that Paré applied a history-making innovation in surgery which has ever since been associated with his name. To prevent bleeding after an amputation, surgeons usually applied a hot cautery to the cut ends of the main blood vessels, inducing the blood to clot. Any mild surface infection at the site of the wound, however, would loosen the clot, and many amputated patients bled to death from the reopened ends of the vessels. Paré adopted the simple device of tying off the ends of the vessels with linen thread—what is now known as a ligature.

Shortly after this campaign he was appointed a surgeon-in-ordinary to King Henry II. An appeal for his help soon came from the besieged city of Metz, where a French garrison was surrounded by a Spanish army. Nearly all the wounded in the city died, and it was thought that the medicaments being used to treat them might be poisoned. Paré made his way into the city through the Spanish lines with the help of a Spanish-speaking servant. After surveying the situation he concluded that the cause of the high mortality was the severity of the wounded's injuries, abetted by the extreme cold. He succeeded in saving many lives with skillful dressing of wounds and common-sense treatment.

The following year Paré was captured by the Spaniards at Hesdin in Picardy. He avoided being put to death on the battlefield by attaching himself, disguised as a servant, to a French nobleman who was considered an important prisoner by the Spaniards. The nobleman had suffered a bullet wound through the lungs. Paré knew that his patient was dying and feared that he would be blamed, so he was delighted when he was ordered to hand over the treatment of his charge to a Spanish charlatan. When the nobleman died, Paré was asked to embalm the body. He did this with such skill and so shrewd a display of anatomical knowledge that he was asked to enter the Spaniards' service under the Duke of Savoy. This he had the courage to refuse. Ultimately Paré regained his liberty by saving the life of another wounded nobleman. During his service under Charles IX of France, Paré performed one of his less creditable experiments. A substance known as "bezoar stone"—a calcium growth which sometimes forms in the intestines of goats and other ruminant animals—was supposed at the time to be an almost magical antidote to all poisons. Paré, who refused to believe this, was challenged to prove that bezoar stone was ineffective. He accepted the challenge and chose as the subject of his experiment an unfortunate cook who was to be hanged for the theft of two silver plates. The cook was given corrosive sublimate, followed by the useless bezoar, and died in great agony. Paré performed a triumphant post-mortem examination which proved that the bezoar had failed to counteract the effects of corrosive sublimate.

Between military campaigns Paré pursued his studies of anatomy in Paris. For these he used the body of an executed criminal, of which he dissected only one side. He claimed to have kept this half-dissected corpse for more than 27 years, but gave no details of his method of preservation. Working with his friend, Thierry de Hery, Paré published a small treatise on anatomy in 1549, six years after his great contemporary Vesalius had published the famous *Fabrica*. Paré's treatise could not have owed much to the *Fabrica*, since the barber-surgeon was ignorant of Latin. The most important section of his book was an appendix on obstetrics and gynecology. It is plain to any medical reader of this section today that Paré must have based it on a great deal of firsthand experience and observation.

In the course of a chapter on surgical extraction of a child from the womb "whether dead or alive," Paré almost casually reported an obstetrical discovery of the first importance. He described a procedure for turning the fetus by drawing down the feet so that it can be extracted without injury to the mother. This maneuver, now known as "podalic version," is one of Paré's greatest contributions to medical practice.

Paré's reputation in Europe eventually became so outstanding that the physicians and surgeons of Paris elected him to their faculties without the usual examinations or fees, in spite of his lack of Latin and Greek. He went on publishing books, of which his most important was *Five Books of Surgery*, retired from military campaigns, and spent most of his time working in Paris, with the title of "premier surgeon of the King." Paré was encouraged by this title to attempt to gain personal control over all the surgeons working in France, but this met with defeat.

In 1573 Paré's wife died. She had borne him three children, only one of whom, a daughter, survived to adult years. Though now 64, Paré soon married again, and his second wife, Jacqueline Rousselet, bore him six more children. Two of them were boys, but both died in infancy.

In 1575 he brought together all his writings and published them in a single volume, the *Collected Works*. The learned physicians and surgeons of Paris, still jealous of him though they had elected him to their company, saw an opportunity to attack in the fact that the Oeuvres were not written in Latin; Paré replied briefly in a published note that Hippocrates, the father of medicine, also had written in his own language. Not handicapped by false modesty, the great surgeon knew that his book was the most enlightened surgical work ever published up to that time. During his lifetime three more editions of his work were published, and it was translated into Dutch, German and Latin. His splendid book was so full of improvements in the theory and practice of surgery that it remained the leading authority on the subject throughout Europe for many years.

Paré's contributions were not confined to surgery. He invented instruments for extracting bullets and arrowheads from wounds, for holding open the mouth of a person suffering from lockjaw so that he could be fed, for extracting teeth. He was the first to suggest the reimplantation of teeth knocked out of the jaws. He introduced the use of artificial limbs and popularized the use of trusses for hernia. He presented original medical descriptions of congenital "monsters," such as Siamese twins. He was even responsible for the first important work on medical jurisprudence.

Paré passed the last 15 years of his life living quietly in Paris. But at the age of 80 he emerged from seclusion for one final act on behalf of the common people from whom he had sprung. The city, in rebellion against the King of Navarre, was being besieged and its citizens were dying of famine. They wished to surrender, but the city's commander, the Archbishop of Lyons, answered their demands with bloodshed. Paré rose to protest against the commander's cruelty. Because of his great prestige, his plea for a peaceful settlement prevailed. Paré died soon afterward, on December 20, 1590, and he was buried in the Church of Saint Andre des Arts.

The Late Joseph Lister: The Father of Antiseptic Surgery

By John B. Huber, A. M. , M. D.

For a just appreciation of the life work of Joseph Baron Lister, we should first consider what surgery was before he began his epoch-making career, and until his discovery had gained the general acceptance of his colleagues.

Before the coming of anesthesia, the elder sister of antisepsis, in 1846, the surgical field was, by comparison with its expanse today, exceedingly limited. Those who operated were men whose knowledge of the human anatomy was well nigh perfect, men of marvelous skill and courage; they oftentimes thrilled the amphitheater where they worked to tremendous excitement; it is written (nor need we doubt the record) that patients collapsed and died "on the table" of terror at the first incision; operations were amazingly rapid, by reason that the patient had to suffer, without relief, the psychic shock and the frightful agony, inflicted by the knife, the saw and the necessary manipulations. Every second saved was incalculably precious. In these circumstances there was naturally lacking the exquisite technic characteristic of present-day surgery; for the lethal state of the patient now precludes the necessity of haste. But all such shock and torture were obviated for the patient when the dentist Morton successfully gave ether in the Massachusetts General Hospital on October 16th, 1846, the date now appropriately celebrated in Boston as "Ether Day" and almost simultaneous with this came the discovery of chloroform by the Scotchman Simpson.

But even the blessed advent of anesthesia by no means rid surgery of all its terrors; to this end she needed the aid of her younger sister antisepsis. The torture of the operation was abolished; but there was dreadful after suffering, and all too frequently did death follow. Those who served in hospitals had to dress wounds after operation—wounds reeking with pus, gangrenous, and saturated with the germs of erysipelas, tetanus, pyemia and septicemia. Then did hospital fever reap its dreadful harvest. In those rare cases when "primary union" was obtained; without a drop of pus, without fever and with but little torture to the patient, it was rightly held to be a wonerderful achievement. Such was the status of surgery before 1870–about the time of Lister's first demonstration of his methods of antisepsis.

Every great discovery is, as it were, the apex of a pyramid; it is the culmination, in the genius of an innovator, of the thought and contributions of many preceding laborers in the devoted service of mankind. As early as 1840, Semmelweiss, in Vienna, considered puerperal fever an infectious disease, though he could not prove it in the present-day sense; in the hospitals of that city women in childbirth were dying in enormous numbers because of the infected atmosphere of these institutions–but even more so, it would seem, by reason that physicians coming from cases of scarlet fever or dipththeria or typhus were not scrupulous in such ordinary precautions of cleanliness, as the washing of their hands. Semmelweiss practised strict cleanliness and the use of calcium chloride, and thus reduced the death rate among his own cases from 12 to 1.2 per cent. The contemporaries in his profession were merciless in their scorn and abuse of him; he had offered a boon and had naturally expected its loyal acceptance by his unwashed colleagues; his sensitive soul broke down under the vituperation he received instead, and he died in a madhouse. More fortunate in his advocacy of similar views was Oliver Wendell Holmes, the great physician and philosopher. Holmes, in 1843, maintained, as did Semmelweiss, the infectiousness of puerperal fever. In 1844 Litzmann characterized it as "a febrile miasmo-contagious disease peculiar to puerperal women." Yet so slowly are such lessons learned that even recent years have not infrequently been their cases of this dreadful disease; and it is computed that between 1816 and 1875 Europe had 170,000 cholera deaths, 165,000 variola deaths and 363,600 deaths from childbed fever.

Tyndall noted (as might anyone else) that solar light, in passing through a dark room, reveals its track by illuminating the dust floating in the air; but with the intuition of genius (which everyone has not) he recalled the statement of Daniel Culverwell that "the sun discovers atomes, though they be insensible by candle light, and makes them dance naked in his beams." Tyndall, in his researches on the decomposition of vapors by light, was compelled to remove these "atomes" and this dust. It was essential for his experiment that the space containing the vapors should contain no visible thing–that no substance capable of scattering the light in the slightest sensible degree should be found in the tube traversed by the luminous beam. He tried ineffectually various means for the elimination of this floating matter, which was *not*, by the way, visible in the exhausted, vacuous experiment tube. But on one occasion, prior to sending the air through the apparatus, he carefully permitted the former to pass over the flame of a spirit lamp; whereupon the floating matter no longer appeared in the experiment tube. It had been burned up by the flame, and was therefore organic matter. Tyndall did not then know the precise nature of this organic matter; but his scientific acumen led him to find here some relation with the researches of such workers as Davaine and Pasteur. Davaine, in France, had in 1863 discovered little rod-like bodies in the blood in wool-sorters' disease (anthrax); and he names these "little rods" "bacteria," after a Greek word descriptive of their shape. This term is now adopted for all germs or micro-organisms. In 1865 Pasteur demonstrated the bacterial origin of pebrine, the silk worm disease, and his finding was violently opposed by those who believed in spontaneous evolution. Tyndall then, for his part, "sensed" that these "atomes" or bacteria or "particulates," as he termed them, were entities not at all identical with units of unvitalized matter. With Pasteur he believed that they were organic and had life; that they were self-multiplying (which phenomenon explains infection); that, however minute they might be, they must partake of the property of vital things and must be differentiated into species, each propagating its own kind and none other. We shall not get figs from thistles, nor thorns from grapes. "If you sow wheat you do not get barley; if you sow smallpox you do not get scarlet fever; the matter of each infectious disease reproduces itself as rigidly as if it were dog or cat."

Such findings as these did Lister infuse with his genius and appropriate to his beneficent ends; it was upon them that he based the principles of antisepsis.

Joseph Lister was graduated in medicine in 1852; from 1869 to 1877 he held the chair of Clinical Surgery in the University of Edinburgh. But years before he began this incumbency he had given thought and had experimented, to the end that germinal infection might be kept from wounds. Carbolic acid was a discovery of that era, and Lister used it as a germicide. His first application of antisepsis was made in the treatment of compound fractures. His conviction was that the impregnated air which reached the wound caused the infection; and he conceived the problem to lie in protecting the wound from the air. He therefore first cleansed the affected region with carbolic acid and then dressed the wound with lint soaked in the acid. His surprising success in this treatment led to its employment in flesh wounds generally and in abscesses. But finding pure carbolic acid unduly irritant and poisonous when absorbed from wounds extensive in area, he next prepared "Lister's antiseptic putty," which was compounded of linseed oil, carbonate of lime and carbolic acid. Here began surgery in the modern sense. Both Tyndall and Pasteur had previously found cotton wool to be an effective means for intercepting bacteria, infusoria and the like, while at the same time germ-free air might pass through. Lister's next important step then was upon this basis to cover wounds not with cotton, but with sterilized gauze. He thus introduced asepsis–exemption from putrefaction.

So, even before the discovery of the bacteria of suppuration (1881), of erysipelas (1883), and tetanus (1887), did Lister prove that by surgical cleanliness all infection could be avoided. The mortality of compound fractures in the pre-antiseptic days was about 60 per cent; it was the most dreaded of all accidents; its mortality now rarely exceeds three per cent, and sepsis (blood poisoning) after such fractures is now practically nil. Before Lister's day the mortality from major operations varied from 50 to 63 per cent; it now seldom exceeds 10 per cent.

Believing that the pathogenic bacteria existed chiefly in the air, Lister prepared apparatus for spraying carbolic acid near the region of the wound; but while such bacteria certainly do exist in this medium, he later found, with others, that the air is not the only (nor, indeed, the chief) source of infection. Unsterilized dressings, sponges, instruments, clothing, were also discovered to be sources of putrefaction. So the use of the spray was abandoned; and the most scrupulous "surgical cleanliness" was instituted with regard to any substance that might possibly come in contact with a wound. The surgeon now seeks to be rid not only of the dirt that can be seen, but also of the microscopic dirt that cannot be seen. No one can touch a wound howsoever lightly with ordinarily clean hands without infecting it.

After eight years of teaching, which was oftentimes received with an "indulgent smile"; after eight years of operations, amazingly successful, based upon the antiseptic principle, Lister's views were accepted and followed in Scotland, "after a fashion." He was much more appreciated in Germany and America than in England. And we may well agree with Dr. Keen, who wrote a decade ago that "when the profession arose en masse, within the last few years, at the International Congress of Berlin, and at the meeting of the British Medical Association in Montreal, and welcomed him with cheer after cheer, it was but a feeble expression of gratitude for benefits which no words can express."

The infectionless operation, coupled with anesthesia, has increased the range of surgery beyond the wildest dreams of those who labored in this field but thirty years ago. Here is a merciful revolution which only he who has lived through the old surgery into the new can appreciate. Our amputations and compound fractures are now practically without danger.

As to tumors: Sir Astley Cooper was most reluctant to remove so simple a thing as a wen from the august pate of George the Fourth, for fear a possibly fatal erysipelas might supervene. Today tumors in all parts of the body (even those involved in a most tortuous cervical labyrinth of vital vessels and nerves) are removed. Bone deformities following fracture are refractured, the deformed portions removed, or joined end to end, and all with little fever and no suppuration.

Until within a few years past, fractures and other injuries of the skull have been invariably dangerous and the most fatal of all accidents. Now, unless the sufferer is instantly killed, there is much hope of his recovery. For example, Dr. Fluhner of this city operated upon a gun shot wound in which the ball entered at the forehead, traversed the entire cranium, was deflected by the occiput, pursued its further course downward into the brain; the back of the skull was trephined, the ball was found and removed. A drainage tube was passed through the entire brain from front to rear, and the patient recovered. Many tumors have been successfully removed from the brain, and more marvelous still, many brain abscesses have been healed through modern surgery. No region of the human body is now safe from the surgeon's knife. The thorax is frequently entered; and even wounds of the heart are now repeatedly sewed up, with recovery. The opening of the abdomen and the pelvis are now the commonest experience of the surgeon, who has much less fear of such proceeding than Sir Astley Cooper had of removing that wen from the royal scalp.

Such is the status of modern surgery. We now address the great Englishman formally as Joseph, Baron Lister–a good title; but generations hence many thousands of sufferers, on being triumphantly relieved, will have in grateful memory no other insignia than that of Joseph Lister, the Father of Antiseptic Surgery.

Section 5: Medical Devices

5.1 The Medical Influence of the Stethoscope
By Stanley Joel Reiser

5.2 The Origins of Hypodermic Medication
By Norman Howard-Jones

The Medical Influence of the Stethoscope

By Stanley Joel Reiser

In 1816 a young French physician, René Théophile Hyacinthe Laënnec, was called to the bedside of a young woman suffering from the symptoms of heart disease. At that time most physicians arrived at a diagnosis by observing the patient's appearance and questioning the patient about symptoms. Faced with an unusually difficult diagnosis, Laënnec resorted to two little-used methods that involved physical contact with the patient: palpating her body with his hand to feel the underlying structures and rapping her chest with his fingers to generate sounds that would indicate the condition of her internal organs. Both of these efforts were thwarted by the patient's obesity, and the mores of the time prohibited Laënnec from undertaking immediate auscultation: pressing an ear to the chest to hear the sounds of the heart. Stymied, he recalled that sound is amplified when it is transmitted through certain solid bodies. He rolled a sheaf of paper into a cylinder and, placing one end on the patient's chest, put his ear to the other end. Through this makeshift instrument he heard more distinct sounds of the action of the heart than he had ever heard before.

Laënnec named his invention the stethoscope, from the Greek *stēthos*, "breast," and *skopein*, "to view." He soon abandoned the roll of paper in favor of what has come to be called the Laënnec stethoscope: a wood cylinder about a foot long and an inch and a half in diameter that could be disassembled into two parts for easy carrying. Running down the long axis of the cylinder was a narrow aperture; in experimenting with different designs Laënnec had discovered that such an aperture enhanced the sound-carrying properties of the instrument. The transmission of certain sounds, such as those of breathing, was further enhanced by a funnel-shaped cavity at the end of the cylinder placed on the patient's chest. If other sounds, such as those of the heart, were to be investigated, a small wood stopper was inserted into the cavity. Realizing that the stethoscope would enable him to hear the sounds generated by the motion of all the organs in the chest, Laënnec set to work to develop a systematic technique of diagnosis based on physical examination with the instrument. As a result of his clear and vigorous presentation of this technique, which he called mediate auscultation, the stethoscope became the first instrument of any kind to be widely used by physicians to diagnose illness.

Diagnosis–the process of determining a patient's disorder from his symptoms–is clearly a crucial step in medical care. The acceptance of the stethoscope led to the establishment of physical examination as the keystone of diagnosis. It worked a profound transformation in the practice of medicine, altering both the physician's perceptions of disease and his relation to the patient. In particular the stethoscope drew the physician for the first time into a private world in which signs were directly communicated to him from the patient's body. It freed the physician to make objective diagnoses, but it also put him at a distance from the personal aspects of illness, opening a gap that is still widening. Indeed, today the stethoscope itself, perhaps the most familiar of all modern medical instruments, has fallen victim to the trend it started toward more objective types of diagnostic technology. To understand how this has come about, consider further the state of medical inquiry before the invention of the stethoscope.

At the beginning of the 19th century diagnoses were made principally on the basis of the patient's verbal account of his illness and the physician's observations (with his unaided senses) of the patient's skin color, tongue condition, breathing and so on. In the 18th century, however, a few manual techniques–methods of diagnostic exploration based on physical examination–had begun to attract attention. One of the most significant, in terms of the changing attitude toward clinical diagnosis, was the technique of percussion that Laënnec had used on his patient with the heart disorder: striking the body to generate sounds that would indicate the vitality of the internal organs.

Percussion was the invention of the Viennese physician Leopold Auenbrugger, who first described it in his *Inventum novum*, a small monograph published in 1761. Auenbrugger pointed out, as Laënnec would 58 years later, that the physician's observations of the external signs of illness were of little use in the diagnosis of chest disease. Patients with the same disorder often exhibited different symptoms, and patients with different disorders often exhibited the same symptoms. Auenbrugger was also critical of the patient's own account of his symptoms, which he considered variable and untrustworthy. For Auenbrugger it was the morbid sound he himself elicited by percussing a patient that was the most dependable index of the nature and course of chest disease, and in *Inventum novum* he proclaimed his ability to diagnose (to translate from the Latin) "from the testimony of my own senses."

Auenbrugger was concerned with finding objective evidence of disease, and he believed that the technique of percussion, which minimized the importance of the personality and physical appearance of the patient, would revolutionize the diagnosis of chest disorders, giving physicians a dependable alternative to their usual untrustworthy methods of diagnosis. Unfortunately Auenbrugger's technique of inferring the nature of an internal abnormality from the character of the sound created in striking the chest was in such strong opposition to reigning medical theory that in his lifetime percussion never gained the attention it deserved.

To appreciate percussion a physician had to think of disease in anatomical terms, explaining the genesis of symptoms in a patient in relation to structural changes in the tissues of the body. This picture of disease was highly unorthodox in the mid-18th century, when most physicians still held to the ancient Greek view that illness was caused by an imbalance in the basic body fluids known as humors. An interest in normal anatomy and its structural transformation through disease had been developing since the 16th century, when revolutionary treatises such as Vesalius' *De humani corporis fabrica* were published, but 18th-century physicians still thought anatomical abnormalities were of secondary importance in gaining an understanding of the genesis of disease and the generation of symptoms. A work that would profoundly influence physicians to think in terms of anatomy, the Italian anatomist Giovanni Battista Morgagni's *De sedibus et causis morborum per anatomen indagatis* (*The Seats and Causes of Diseases Discovered by Anatomy*), was published the same year as Auenbrugger's *Inventum novum* and therefore had little effect on the early reactions to percussion. (By the time Laënnec began to promote mediate auscultation, however, efforts such as Auenbrugger's and Morgagni's had resulted in a somewhat more favorable attitude toward anatomical explanations of disease.)

The lack of enthusiasm for percussion also had to do with Auenbrugger's manner of presentation. The variations in percussive sounds by which diseases can be discriminated are subtle. To learn how to apply the method the physician needed extensive descriptions and many examples of these complex acoustic phenomena. In Auenbrugger's brief treatise he chose to give only terse, vague explanations, trusting that his discovery would be valued "by those who can firstly appreciate medical science." Indeed, he refused to elaborate on his technique for skeptics or critics, whom he judged to be "beset by envy, malice, detraction and calumny."

Auenbrugger's technique of percussion did have several failings. For example, it was not effective with patients whose disorders were located deep within the chest cavity. The comparison of healthy and morbid sounds in the same patient was an important part of diagnosis by percussion, and so the technique also did not work well with patients who had two diseased lungs. Modern physicians who employ percussion put the fingers of one hand on a patient's body to soften the percussive blow, but the form of percussion Auenbrugger advocated was harsher, requiring that the physician deliver a blow directly to the patient's body with the tips of all the fingers on one hand. This procedure could be quite distressing to the patient, and some physicians refused to employ it for that reason. Moreover, at that time any manual activity was generally considered to be beneath the dignity of the physician. In particular the physical intimacy required by percussion threatened to undermine the professional standing of the physician, even to place him in a class with the surgeon, over whom he affirmed both medical and social superiority.

In his time Laënnec was confronted with much the same kind of medical and social resistance to manual physical examination that Auenbrugger had faced in the mid-18th century. There had been one significant change in the medical climate in the time between the introduction of percussion and the introduction of mediate auscultation. By 1816 physicians were generally willing to believe specific anatomical defects were dependable hallmarks of certain disorders and could be exploited to differentiate among diseases. In particular the correlation of the symptoms in the living patient and the structural changes found in the body at autopsy was beginning to play an important part in the discovery and verification of medical facts (and in the training of physicians). Therefore Laënnec could demonstrate through autopsy that when sounds of a certain kind were heard in the chest, lesions of a certain kind were found in the cadaver.

Like Auenbrugger, Laënnec believed a set of audible signs could be the basis of a new and more dependable technique of diagnosis. He spent three years at the Necker Hospital in Paris auscultating healthy subjects and sick ones, listening to the murmurs, rales (crackling sounds), wheezes and burbles inside their chest and performing autopsies in order to identify and classify the sounds. In 1819 he published *Traite de la auscultation mediate* (*On Mediate Auscultation*), a comprehensive critique of the diagnostic methods of the time that culminated in an exhaustive description of the technique of mediate auscultation. The treatise is a meticulous exploration of the connections between the sounds generated within the body and specific anatomical defects and diseases. Some 10 times longer than Auenbrugger's monograph on percussion, Laënnec's work contains descriptions of sound that surpass in clarity most that have appeared since. "When the patient coughed or spoke, and still more during respiration," wrote Laënnec in one case study, "there was heard a tinkling like that of a small bell which has just stopped ringing or of a gnat buzzing within a porcelain vase." Such vivid descriptions had much to do with the success of mediate auscultation in gaining the attention and respect of a wide audience of physicians.

Initially physicians found a variety of reasons to criticize the technique. Some thought they would appear ludicrous, bent over the bodies of their patients listening for sounds through an instrument that resembled a divining rod. And there was still the concern that the use of instruments and manual techniques was beneath the station of the physician. The transporting of medical instruments was particularly disturbing, and some physicians resorted to such expedients as carrying the two disassembled parts of the stethoscope crossed inside their top hat. (This particular practice was not without its perils: on one occasion, when a snowball knocked off a medical student's top hat and revealed a stethoscope, the student was charged with carrying a concealed weapon.)

Furthermore, many physicians found the views of the early proponents of the stethoscope extreme. In *On Mediate Auscultation* Laënnec judged the standard methods–even the manual techniques–of the day harshly, finding palpation "too vague and uncertain to be of much benefit" and percussion only slightly more valuable. He was also critical of the ancient practice of pulse taking, explaining its popularity by pointing out that the procedure inconvenienced neither the physician nor the patient, and that any particular irregularity was subject to a wide range of interpretations. Laënnec and many of his followers maintained that authoritative diagnoses could be made principally–indeed, sometimes exclusively–on the basis of aural information. Other less partisan physicians believed the most reliable diagnosis could be arrived at by giving equal consideration to aural signs and information gained through traditional methods; they were understandably annoyed by the uncompromising views of Laënnec and his followers. Actually the excessive claims made for the stethoscope were due in part to Laënnec's extraordinary abilities. Having remarkably acute hearing and a precise knowledge of the pathological meaning of the most delicate variations in sound, he could distinguish diseases on the basis of auscultatory information with wonderful accuracy. Few of Laënnec's followers appreciated how unusual his skill was.

The reactions of patients to the stethoscope were generally favorable, although some were frightened by the device (associating instruments with surgeons) or embarrassed by the physical closeness of the physician required by auscultation. Some patients refused to be examined with the stethoscope because of the excessive force with which their physician pressed the instrument against them or because of the inconvenience of having to make frequent changes in position during such an examination. What patients feared most, however, was the accuracy of the stethoscope. Often it converted a last hope that an illness was remediable into a certainty that it was not.

In the final analysis, of course, the great strengths of mediate auscultation were just this accuracy and dependability: the technique could convert diagnostic suspicions into diagnostic certainties. As Laënnec and his followers pointed out, having confidence in a diagnosis meant that diseases could be treated with new vigor. Therapies could be applied promptly, in some cases at early stages of illness. And even if the disease diagnosed was incurable, the patient could at least be spared useless and perhaps painful therapy.

The accuracy of diagnoses made with the stethoscope resulted in a growing public acceptance of mediate auscultation. In fact, within a decade of the publication of *On Mediate Auscultation* popular sentiment in favor of the technique had become so strong that a physician who did not employ the stethoscope jeopardized his professional reputation. Some physicians who did not know how to auscultate patients took to carrying stethoscopes with them for display purposes. Physical examination–through auscultation–was the new mode of diagnosis.

In the second half of the 19th century many improvements were made in the rigid, monaural Laënnec stethoscope. To accommodate physicians who resented carrying such a bulky object smaller stethoscopes were developed. Changes in the design of the instrument (for example the substitution of a parabolic cavity for the conical one at the end to be placed on the patient's chest) improved its acoustic properties. As early as 1829 the first stethoscope that was not completely rigid was built by an Edinburgh physician named Nicholas Comins. The instrument consisted of two rigid wood tubes, each one about seven inches long, connected by a joint so that they could be set at any angle; an earpiece attached to one of the tubes also rotated about a joint.

Fully flexible monaural stethoscopes made of pliable tubing first appeared in the 1830's. These instruments, which could be up to two and a half feet long, spared patients having to change position repeatedly during an examination and the discomfort of a rigid instrument pushed against them. Moreover, with a flexible stethoscope patients were no longer forced into such close contact with the physician; a woman could place the cup of the flexible stethoscope on her body herself, thereby keeping the physician at a proper distance. Similarly, physicians could avoid close contact with patients who had contagious diseases. They were also spared the discomfort of bending to examine patients (a particular boon for fat physicians), and they could even auscultate themselves.

Comins was probably also the first to suggest the binaural stethoscope: a flexible stethoscope with tubes going to both ears. It was not until the early 1850's, however, that the first satisfactory working models were introduced. In 1878, when the microphone was invented, an even greater amplification of body sounds seemed possible, but it was soon evident that the heart and lung sounds picked up by the microphone were not clear enough for diagnostic purposes.

The initial excitement and later disappointment over the microphone coincided with the introduction of a large number of different types of stethoscope, and much confusion resulted. Physicians began to worry that any amplification would alter the sounds to which they had become accustomed. Many chose to ignore the vast array of different stethoscopes, insisting that it was the learning of the physician that mattered in auscultation. not the instrument he wielded. As a result the acoustically superior (and handily carried) flexible binaural stethoscope was not generally adopted until the 1890's. In the early 1900's physicians realized that a diaphragm stretched over the mouth of the cup of the stethoscope would enhance the transmission of certain kinds of sounds, and so this feature was added to the instrument. Modern stethoscopes follow the same basic design and generally have two cups: one bell-shaped cup without a diaphragm for transmitting sounds of lower pitch and a wider, flatter cup with a diaphragm for transmitting sounds of higher pitch.

Paradoxically the acceptance of the binaural stethoscope coincided with the discovery of a device that would quickly displace the stethoscope as the preeminent tool in the diagnosis of chest disease. In 1895 W. K. Röntgen discovered that a cathode-ray tube emitted radiation that could pass through a solid object and fix the image of the object's internal structure on a photographic plate. News of Röntgen's discovery of these X rays, a "new kind of light which penetrated and photographed everything," spread quickly. The X-ray picture he had made of his wife's hand was reproduced in publications all over the world, and newspapers competed with one another in publishing exaggerated accounts of the potential uses of the discovery. The general public avidly bought X-ray images of their loved ones' hand and of ordinary objects such as keys taken through an opaque container such as a purse. (The queen of Portugal had X-ray pictures made of all the members of her court; the distorted rib cages disclosed by the X rays led some of the female members to discard their tightly laced corsets.)

Physicians were immensely enthusiastic about Röntgen's discovery and quickly applied X rays to the diagnosis of bone fractures and kidney stones and to the location of foreign objects such as bullets embedded in body tissue. Within a month of the discovery an apparatus was in use that projected X rays through a patient's body onto a fluorescent screen so that the physician could even directly observe lung and heart motions. As X-ray techniques improved it became possible to analyze disorders within the softer tissues of the body such as the lungs and the heart.

With X rays physicians could often discern lung and heart disorders earlier and define their character more accurately than they could with a stethoscope. In 1896 the pioneering radiologist Francis H. Williams expressed the sentiments of many other physicians when he wrote: "We may now look where we have previously only been able to listen and sometimes to hear but imperfectly." To many the transformation of auscultatory sounds into images in the mind of the physician seemed less reliable than the direct analysis of defects displayed in X-ray pictures. Patients too had more confidence in a diagnosis based on an anatomical defect they could see in a picture. The use of the stethoscope began to decline, a trend that was accelerated in the 20th century by the development of more sophisticated types of diagnostic technology such as the electrocardiograph. Indeed. as physicians became increasingly captivated with diagnostic technology they became less concerned with physical examination in general and with the techniques developed in the 19th century for accomplishing it.

Today the stethoscope is the old warrior of medicine. Although it cannot compete with the array of elaborate and expensive technologies for which it paved the way, it clings tenaciously, resisting retirement. Its staying power in modern times is based in part on its giving both physicians and patients a sense of continuity with the past. Identified with dependable diagnosis, the familiar object evokes confidence. Most important. it provides those physicians who still know how to use it with good, immediate and low-cost information that can eliminate the need for complicated diagnostic tests.

It is, of course, easy for the modern physician to refer his patient to a clinical laboratory or X-ray department for diagnostic tests instead of conducting an intensive examination with a stethoscope. Such tests are usually covered by insurance policies, so that there is little immediate cost to the patient and the physician saves time. Indeed, as fewer physicians are trained in methods such as auscultation, choosing the high-technology route is only prudent. What is lost is primarily the self -reliance of the physician. When the 19th-century physician chose to make diagnoses less on patients' verbal accounts of their symptoms and more on the physical signs of illness that in many cases he alone detected, he was obliged to make up his own mind about illness. As a medical era the 20th century must be characterized as a time when physicians have come to rely less on themselves and more on specialists, technicians and machines to collect and evaluate the evidence of disease.

The Origins of Hypodermic Medication

By Norman Howard-Jones

The hypodermic syringe shares with the stethoscope the distinction of being almost a symbol of the practicing physician. There must be few people with access to medical care who have not received a hypodermic injection to protect them from disease or to give rapid relief from pain. Millions of diabetics have been taught to give themselves daily hypodermic injections of insulin.

The main advantages of this method of administering drugs, which takes its name from the Greek words meaning under the skin, are that the active principles are quickly absorbed into the bloodstream from the subcutaneous tissue and that they are not altered or destroyed by the digestive juices. These advantages were not, however, what the Scottish physician Alexander Wood had in mind when he introduced the procedure in 1853. He intended it as a means of anesthetizing peripheral nerves and thereby relieving pain in patients with neuralgia. Another peculiarity in the history of this method of administering drugs was that for many years it was not recognized that the hypodermic injection of morphine, which was regarded as a harmless substitute for taking the drug orally in the form of opium, was the equal of or the superior to opium-eating in producing drug addiction. A third curiosity in this strange story is that nearly all the standard histories of medicine attribute the introduction of hypodermic medication to the wrong man, the French physician Charles Gabriel Pravaz.

A noteworthy feature of the opening two decades of the 19th century was the isolation for the first time of the active principles of a number of drugs, most of them alkaloids. They included morphine, atropine, strychnine and many less familiar compounds. The availability of compounds that were highly active in minute doses was a stimulus to the search for new methods of administering them.

In 1809 the French physiologist François Magendie, who experimented with animals in various ways in an effort to elucidate physiological processes, administered a Javanese arrow poison to dogs by coating the point of a wooden barb with it and thrusting it into the rump. The effects were lethal. The active principle of this poison was subsequently found to be strychnine. (Magendie's venture may well have been the first step in experimental pharmacology. Later another arrow poison, curare, used by primitive South American tribes, was to become a valuable aid in modern anesthesiology.)

The notion of administering drugs through the skin gained ground slowly. In 1825 the French physician A. J. Lesieur published an account of what he termed the "endermic method." It consisted of the application of a vesicant to blister the epidermis; then the drug–usually one of the recently isolated alkaloids–was applied to the denuded skin as a powder, a solution or an ointment. Six years later Sir Robert Christison, a Scottish physician, suggested that whales might be killed by fastening a phial of prussic acid to a harpoon "in such a way that the phial should break when a strain was put upon the harpoon after entering the body of the animal."

In 1836 the French physician G. V. Lafargue took a further step toward hypodermic medicine as it is now known. In papers read first in Paris to the Academy of Sciences and then to the Academy of Medicine he described how, after using the Lesieur method, he conceived the idea of introducing morphine under the skin by means of a vaccination lancet. The point of the lancet was dipped in morphine and then forced almost horizontally under the skin. After a few seconds it was withdrawn. Although Lafargue regarded his inoculation primarily as a form of local medication, he did pose the question of whether or not the morphine so administered might have a general action on the organism. He did not, however, pursue the idea.

In 1859, after Wood's method had become known, the French physician Louis Jules Behier published an account of his own experience with hypodermic medication. He had used a syringe that differed from the one employed by Wood, and he called it the "Pravaz apparatus." Pravaz had used this type of syringe to inject chemical coagulants into the blood vessels of animals (he was trying to find a treatment for aneurysm in humans) but never for hypodermic medication either in his patients or in animals. Nevertheless, Behier's use of Pravaz' name led to the belief that it was he who had invented the hypodermic syringe and introduced hypodermic medication into practice. (In 1927 *La Presse Medicale*, the leading French medical weekly, reported a campaign to save the memory of Pravaz from oblivion by erecting a monument in his native village to "the father of the hypodermic method.")

As interest in the hypodermic injection of medicaments grew in France, Lafargue came on the scene again to raise a dissenting voice. He felt, he wrote in 1861, that he should break the silence about "Wood's method." Syringes were costly and delicate; they deteriorated rapidly, and handling them required a deft touch. Only a few physicians had them, and few patients had had or would be likely to have the opportunity of benefiting from Wood's method. Lafargue proposed an alternative method, which he called "hypodermic inoculation by plugging." It consisted of inserting medicated pellets under the skin by procedures that now seem rather bizarre. The skin was pierced–a darning needle would do the job, according to Lafargue–and the pellet was inserted with the fingers or with tweezers. The puncture was then covered with a piece of stamp paper or whatever other adhesive might be ready to hand. Lafargue also devised a kind of implantation gun, which he called a dry syringe. (The implantation of solid pellets reappeared as an original discovery in 1937, when two British workers described a technique for implanting in animals tablets containing hormones. The method was briefly employed in Britain and the U.S. in the treatment of human patients.)

As late as 1873 physicians were exercising their ingenuity to find new techniques for the subcutaneous administration of drugs. In that year the British physician J. M. Crombie, giving as his justification "the dearness and delicacy of the syringe," advocated the use of morphine-impregnated silk threads slowly drawn through two perforations in the skin by means of a suitable needle. Neither this method nor the others survived the competition of hypodermic injection.

It cannot be said that the search for new methods of administering drugs had a sound scientific basis. The new alkaloids had been discovered; they undoubtedly had a powerful effect on the human organism, and doctors were determined to use them. Wood wrote in 1858 of having tried strychnine in neuralgia. He said he had cured a case, "but I never tried it again, for it seemed likely to kill two people: my patient, an old lady, who nearly died of the poison; and myself, then a young doctor, who nearly died of fright." Behier preferred to treat neuralgia with massive doses of atropine. He dispassionately described the side effects, which included malaise, dizziness and hallucinations.

Most of the therapeutic results claimed by the early users of hypodermic medication are so inconsistent with the present knowledge of the pharmacological action of the drugs administered that scant reliance can be placed on any of the observations made. This skepticism is fully justified by the astonishing claims made in the latter years of the 19th century for the injection of pure water as a therapeutic procedure. A French physician, L. Lafitte, read a paper on the subject in 1875. After seeing, as he recounts, the "miraculous and immediate manner" in which several hypodermic injections of water, administered by his then chief in 1872, had "cured or relieved" the symptoms of a boy with acute articular rheumatism, Lafitte employed the treatment systematically. "Always," he says, "success sanctioned my trials." He thought that water exerted a physical action on nerve endings and suggested that it should replace morphine.

This communication was followed by letters from several physicians who had also been practicing this remarkable form of hydrotherapy. One of them, E. Lelut, explains how he had unwittingly injected water into a patient with sciatica who had previously been receiving morphine injections. The next day the patient thanked Lelut effusively, saying: "Doctor, how grateful I am to you! You relieved my pain today without upsetting my stomach." Lelut thought he had injected a solution of morphine, but on investigating the unusually satisfying therapeutic result he found that the hired girl had upset the bottle containing the morphine solution and, to cover her traces, had substituted plain water. He adds that since this happy experience he has employed nothing but water for injections. In the years that followed many papers were published on the therapeutic value of water administered by hypodermic injection.

Ten years before Wood published the first account of hypodermic injection an Irish physician, F. Rynd, gave an account of a method that came very near to it. On May 5, 1844, a woman aged 59 was admitted to the Meath Hospital and County Dublin Infirmary. From Rynd's description she would appear to have been suffering from pain involving the trigeminal nerve of the face. Rynd states, rather cryptically, that on June 3 "a solution of fifteen grains of acetate of morphia, dissolved in one drachm of creosote [!], was introduced to the supra-orbital nerve, and along the course of the temporal, malar and buccal nerves, by means of an instrument made for the purpose." As is so often the case with new medical treatments, the result was regarded as a success.

It was not until 1861 that Rynd published a description of the instrument he had used. It was essentially a kind of hollow needle through which the morphine solution was introduced by gravity. It was typical of the rather brash claims to priority of the time that Rynd stated: "The subcutaneous injection of fluids, for the relief of neuralgia, was first practised in this country [then meaning the British Isles] by me, in the Meath Hospital, in the month of May, 1844." (He seemed to have forgotten that in his original publication in 1845 he had given June as the month.)

Rynd's gravity-flow method was not hypodermic injection as it is now known. The true innovator was Wood, whose first description of the method, published in 1855, was titled "New Method of Treating Neuralgia by the direct application of Opiates to the Painful Points." The title expresses the essence of Wood's idea: injecting morphine hypodermically to induce a local analgesia at tender points in a nerve.

Wood was apparently unaware of Rynd's 1845 publication. Since it had appeared in the *Dublin Medical Press*, which was far from being a leading British medical periodical, Wood's lack of knowledge of it is not surprising. Wood was influenced by observations made in France by François-Louis-Isidore Valleix that sensitive points could be detected along nerves in cases of neuralgia. Valleix used the technique of blistering the skin over such points with vesicants and then applying a solution of morphine to the broken surface. Wood had the idea that he could apply the morphine more directly to the affected nerve by using "one of the elegant little syringes constructed ... by Mr Ferguson of Giltspur Street, London." These syringes were intended for the injection of chemical coagulants into birthmarks; the idea was that the coagulants would close the blood vessels and result in a less unsightly birthmark. Wood said it had occurred to him that the syringe "might supply the means of bringing some narcotic to bear more directly than I had been able to accomplish on the affected nerve in neuralgia."

Fired with this notion, Wood decided to try his new method on an elderly spinster whose "cervico-brachial neuralgia" prevented her from sleeping. He ascertained the most tender spot and injected subcutaneously about two-fifths of a grain of a salt of morphine. This was a heroic dose that cured the patient's insomnia, if nothing else, for at least one night. Indeed, Wood, visiting her the next morning, was "a little annoyed to find that she had never wakened; the breathing was also somewhat deep, and she was roused with difficulty."

It is rather extraordinary that notwithstanding this incident Wood continued to be convinced that hypodermic injection had a purely local effect on the nerves. It is also odd to read today that for his historic first injection he used sherry as a solvent for the morphine. "I thought that it would not irritate and smart so much as alcohol," he said, "and ... it would not rust the instrument as a water solution of opium would do."

By 1858 Wood had improved on the Ferguson syringe by graduating the barrel and by using a finer needle, which caused less damage to the tissue. In the *British Medical Journal* of October 23, 1858, an advertisement appeared for "Dr. Alexander Wood's Narcotic Injection Syringes." His second paper, published in 1858 and giving particulars of the improved syringe, attracted considerably more attention than the first one had and resulted in an extension of the use of the hypodermic method beyond the Scottish border.

In 1858 Wood was still dominated by the idea of a local action of morphine on the peripheral nerves. He maintained that the injection should be made not at the site of the pain but at a point found to be tender on pressure. He told of a woman with neuralgic pains whom he had "punctured upwards of one hundred times, always in different places; but no sooner had the pain been driven from one spot, than it took up its seat in another." He continued: "At last I had expelled it from every part of the body, except a corner of the head, and there I was puzzled how to deal with it. The fact was, I could detect no painful point in the scalp." For Wood "no painful point" meant no injection, and the woman departed for several months with her husband to take a cure at the German baths. On her return Wood examined her twice, and on the second occasion he found "the point where the needle should be inserted." According to Wood, this final "puncture" completed the cure of the woman's neuralgia.

Among those who were stimulated by Wood's second publication to try the subcutaneous injection of medicaments was Charles Hunter, a young London surgeon who in 1858 wrote to the medical press to describe his own experiences with "the local treatment, by narcotic injection into the part." He said that two patients he had treated obtained considerable relief from the local injection of morphine, and he concluded that the narcotic "appears to exert more benefit on the local affection when it has to be absorbed from the part affected itself, probably from being brought more directly into contact with the nerves involved in the disease."

Only two weeks later, however, he wrote again to the medical press with a different conclusion. "I have given up the localisation of the remedy as proposed by Dr Wood," he said, "viz. the injecting of the narcotic into the most painful spot affected by neuralgia." What had happened was that both of the patients had developed abscesses at the site of the injection, and Hunter therefore continued the treatment by injecting morphine in sites remote from the seat of pain. The patients obtained just as much relief as when he injected the drug into the painful area. Hunter accordingly formulated two new conclusions:

> *1. That by the injection of the narcotic into the cellular tissue of a part distant from that affected with the neuralgia, the relief that follows appears quite as great as when the injection is in to the cellular tissue of the neuralgic part. 2. That therefore the idea that relief results from the localisation of the remedy in the painful part is erroneous–equal relief being afforded in either case (injected into the painful part or elsewhere).*

Having made an important discovery, Hunter succumbed to two temptations: he tried to build a therapeutic system around it, and he conceived an exaggerated idea of his own originality. In order to distinguish his "plan" from Wood's he introduced the term "hypodermic. " In 1865 the *London Medical Times & Gazette* endorsed Hunter's claims, saying: "It is now six years [in fact it was seven] since Mr. Hunter proposed the injection of medicines into the cellular tissue with their general therapeutic effect in view. In the case of medicines thus injected for general effects, he called the method 'hypodermic,' to distinguish it from the endermic, and from the local injection of Wood. ... The hypodermic differs from the 'method of Wood.' The latter plan has for its object the local treatment of a local affection. "

Until then Wood had not contested Hunter's claim, but this statement goaded him into a reply that was to lead to an acrimonious and undignified public exchange of correspondence. Writing to the same journal, Wood said that Hunter "is reported to have said 'the hypodermic differs from the method of Wood.' To this I reply that it does so merely in name. I called my method 'subcutaneous,' borrowing from the Latin; Mr Hunter, in appropriating it, called it hypodermic, a Greek compound having precisely the same meaning." Wood insisted that injection into the painful area was often more effective than injection at a remote site. In any case, he said, credit was due the man who "showed the plan of using the cellular tissues as a medium for the introduction of remedies into the system," namely himself.

Hunter riposted: "Does Dr Wood desire to claim a double priority, as to his own theory and practice, and as to one which he admits is a modification, and which is both theoretically and practically different to his plan?" Wood countered by pointing out that he had described general effects in his 1855 publication, adding: "So I did not rest my claim on my *theory* being the correct one." That statement amounted to a tacit admission by Wood that the theoretical basis of his introduction of the subcutaneous injection of medicaments was erroneous. Hunter was not content with such an admission. Wood, he said, "now hankers after more credit … . It was I who first publicly advanced the view … that the localisation of Wood was unnecessary."

At this point the editor closed the correspondence. Many other physicians had joined it, but the editor published only two of their letters. Both took Hunter's part.

In retrospect, and with the benefit of hindslght, Hunter's conclusion that the effect of hypodermic injections of morphine and other alkaloids was general rather than local seems obvious. At the time, however, it was a revolutionary idea. Indeed, it was so revolutionary that the Medical and Chirurgical Society of London appointed a special committee to settle the question. After two years the committee published its findings, which were wholly in favor of Hunter's conclusion.

Had Hunter confined himself to maintaining that the results obtained by Wood's technique were due to a general rather than a local action, he would have been fully vindicated. That he should have put himself forward as the inventor of a new technique, however, seems hardly to have been warranted. It is noteworthy that neither of the protagonists seems to have realized that the injections were not curing a disease but simply alleviating a symptom. Nor did either of them have any concept of the danger of repeated injections of morphine for trivial ailments.

The idea of a local action of hypodermically injected medicine passed into oblivion long ago, but the absence of such an action has never been conclusively proved. More than 20 years ago, when I could find no statement in any standard textbook of pharmacology concerning whether or not morphine had a local action on peripheral nerves, I wrote to the then professor of pharmacology at one of the two ancient English universities. He replied that he would set up experiments to arrive at an answer. I heard nothing further from him. Some doubt therefore remains in my mind whether Wood and later proponents of localization may have been not altogether wrong.

Perhaps the most remarkable blind spot exhibited by the early workers in the field of hypodermic medicine was their failure to foresee the danger that repeated injections of morphine would produce addiction. In 1865 the *London Medical Times & Gazette* reported on a Professor Nussbaum of Munich who, suffering from neuralgia, "had injected morphia under his own skin more than 2000 times–sometimes to the extent of five grains of morphia in twenty-four hours." The journal apparently did not consider the large number of injections and the size of the daily dose worthy of comment.

In the same year the special committee of the Medical and Chirurgical Society reported that "to confirmed opium-eaters this method has been found of much service, smaller doses than those previously taken by mouth being requisite." Hunter recommended morphine injections "as a nerve tonic in cases of great nervous exhaustion, or of irritability or great mental depression." Lafitte, illustrating the popularity of morphine injections, complacently remarked in 1875 that patients commonly cried: "Doctor, doctor, give me an injection quickly; I am suffering like someone possessed; it's my neuralgia, etc."

The first considered warning of the danger of morphinism came in 1870 from Thomas Clifford Allbutt (later Sir Thomas), who subsequently became the Regius Professor of Medicine at the University of Cambridge. "Among the numerous essays and records concerning the hypodermic use of morphia which have been published of late, both at home and abroad," he wrote, "I cannot call to mind one in which its possible dangers have been considered. ... While my fears were indefinite, I felt the time had not come for me to speak. Now my experience has been greater, I have a large number of cases before me, and yet the uncomfortable fear of mischief is growing rather than diminishing." Is it not true, he asked, that doctors are often consulted by patients "who have been injecting themselves daily or more than daily during long periods of time, for neuralgias which seem, nevertheless, as far from cure as they were at the outset?" He then refers to nine patients suffering from "various forms of neuralgia" who all find relief in the "incessant use of the syringe" and who all declare that without the syringe "life would be insupportable."

A hundred years later this picture is all too familiar, with the difference that the early victims of the hypodermic syringe were not sensation-seeking adolescents but mostly respectable Victorian ladies introduced to the habit by their physicians, who were often themselves addicts. Perhaps understandably, it took a long time for Allbutt's warning to be generally heeded.

In later years history was to repeat itself. Morphine injections were first regarded as a harmless substitute for opium-eating. Then heroin and later pethidine were to become "harmless substitutes" for morphine, only to be recognized in time as no less addictive. Barbiturates and amphetamines were to be equally harmless in their turn. The medical profession cannot disclaim all responsibility for the modern scourge of drug addiction.

Another remarkable feature of the early years of hypodermic medication was the absence of any reference to infection resulting from the injection of non-sterile fluids with unsterilized syringes. It was not of course until 1867–12 years after Wood's first publication–that Joseph Lister published his first paper on surgical antisepsis, and the idea that microbial contamination could be responsible for the suppuration of wounds was not accepted for some years.

The early innovators of hypodermic medication were fortunate, as are the many diabetics today who do not get abscesses although their aseptic precautions may be far from perfect. Hunter, whose first two recipients of subcutaneous injections developed infections, was less fortunate in this respect. On the other hand, it was these misfortunes that led him to evolve the "hypodermic plan" as opposed to the "localisation of Wood." Nonetheless, even Hunter maintained in 1865 that if the site of the injection was continually varied and the "puncture" was made "with care and celerity," there was "no fear of abscess or diffuse inflammation."

In the same year Albertus Eulenberg of Germany dismissed as completely groundless the fear of local inflammatory reactions. He supported his contention by reference to a patient whose breast he had injected more than 1,200 times. Fifteen years later Eulenberg admitted that abscesses sometimes occurred, but he maintained that they were "almost exclusively" due to the use of irritant drugs or solvents.

At the same time, however, H. H. Kane in the U.S. left the problem in no doubt. As a result of a questionnaire that he published in "every prominent medical journal of Great Britain, France, Germany and America" he said of morphinisis: "In some of these persons the condition of the body is terrible. Abscesses are to be seen at every stage."

By 1885 the dangers of addiction and infection were generally recognized. The passage of time since Wood had introduced the technique represented a generation. It took that long for the complications attending hypodermic medication to be widely acknowledged by the medical profession.

Section 6: Sexual and Reproductive Health

6.1 Abortion and Contraception in the Middle Ages
By Roland Betancourt

6.2 The Forgotten History of the World's First Trans Clinic
By Brandy Schillace

6.3 The Disturbing History of Research into Transgender Identity
By Jack Turban

6.4 Commentary: The Eugenics Legacy of the Nobelist Who Fathered IVF
By Osagie K. Obasogie

Abortion and Contraception in the Middle Ages

By Roland Betancourt

Today, conversations around abortion in modern Christianity tend to take as a given the longstanding moral, religious and legal prohibition of the practice. Stereotypes of medical knowledge in the ancient and medieval worlds sustain the misguided notion that abortive and contraceptive pharmaceuticals and surgeries could not have existed in the premodern past.

This could not be further from the truth.

While official legal and religious opinions condemned the practice, often citing the health of women, a wealth of medical treatises produced by and for wealthy Christian women across the Middle Ages betray a radically different history–one in which women had a host of pharmaceutical contraceptives, various practices for inducing miscarriages, and surgical procedures for the termination of pregnancies. When it came to saving a woman's life, Christian physicians unhesitatingly recommended these procedures.

Since antiquity, the termination of pregnancies has long been associated with women at the margins of society, such as sex workers, and highlighted not only for the termination of the fetus's life, but for the great danger it posed to women. For instance, in the Hippocratic Oath, Hippocrates refuses to assist in or recommend euthanasia and additionally refuses to give women abortifacients given the danger to which they put the life of the mother.

Religiously, the Church Council of Ancyra in 314 A.D. stated that women found to have committed or attempted an abortion on themselves or others were to be exiled from the Church for 10 years, revising earlier suggestions that they be exiled for life. Yet, in the mid-fourth century, the Church Father Basil the Great revises these decrees, suggesting that time should not be proscriptive but dependent on the repentance of the person. There, however, he focuses not just on the fetus, but again on the danger of these procedures for women, who "usually die from such attempts."

The laws of the early Christian world generally reflected these prohibitions, outlining exile as the punishment for whomever has undertaken an abortion or aided in one–or, death if the person dies in the process. Many of these laws were codified in the sixth-century *Digest* of Justinian, a legal compendium culled from ancient legislative opinions.

Nevertheless, these legal opinions betray the real complexity that abortions had in the ancient and medieval worlds. For example, the *Digest* cites the opinion of the jurist Tryphonius, where a woman was sentenced to death for undertaking an abortion, precisely because she did so with the malicious intent of denying her husband an heir by aborting the unborn inheritor. Legally, we see abortions being intimately associated with a patriarchal control of lineage and reproduction. The *Digest* clarifies that if a woman undertakes an abortion after a divorce, "so as to avoid giving a son to her husband who is now hateful," however, she should only be temporarily exiled.

The fourth-century Church Father John Chrysostom even turned these stereotypes on their head. Though criticizing abortions, in one sermon he offers the example of a sex worker forced to have an abortion so as to not lose her livelihood. While damning the act as a murderous practice, he places blame not on the woman, but on her client, chastising the man by saying that the sex worker cannot be criticized for seeking out an abortion, writing, that while "the shameless act is hers, the cause of it is yours." Thus, it is the sex worker's client who is the cause of the murder, not she who requires her attractive body to survive.

Despite the prohibition in the Hippocratic Oath, gynecological texts were replete with recipes for contraceptive and abortive suppositories. The second-century gynecology of Soranus of Ephesus details these recipes and advocates their use for women who have a medical reason to prevent pregnancy, strongly opposing their use simply "because of adultery or out of a consideration for youthful beauty," given the health risks involved. Thus, adultery and a conceited desire to preserve one's good looks were often lodged against women known to practice abortions.

The recipes of Soranus were transmitted across the centuries in various texts, each demonstrating an active history of use and commentary. For example, in Aëtius of Amida's sixth-century medical treatise, the author details the use of contraceptive vaginal suppositories, elaborating on the improvements to the recipe from Soranus's time. There, Aëtius writes that once the contraceptive has been used, "if she wishes, [the woman] may have intercourse with a man. It is infallible because of its many trials."

Aëtius's gynecological treatise has often been associated with the patronage of the elite imperial circle of Empress Theodora in Constantinople, an empress whom the court historian Procopius once described as often conceiving, "but by using almost all known techniques she could induce immediate miscarriage." The use and efficacy of contraceptives and abortifacients extend throughout the Christian Middle Ages. In one 12th-century text from Salerno, the author offers the example of sex workers, who frequently have intercourse yet only rarely conceive.

Therefore, the medical historical evidence proposes a very different story from that told by official religious or legal texts. The fact of the matter is that good Christian women were indeed undertaking abortions and using contraceptives. Yet, wealthy and elite Christian women had not only recourse to the best medical knowledge of their era but also the privacy to undertake these practices without shame.

Most surprisingly, however, these medical practices were not only relegated to herbal, pharmaceutical contraceptives and abortifacient drugs, but also the various surgical interventions, what today we would refer to as a late-term abortion.

In the early 10th-century *Life of Patriarch Ignatios*, by Nicetas David Paphlagon, a narrative of a religious figure, the author recounts the story of a woman in labor with a breeched birth. There, she is in immense pain and the author writes that "in order to prevent the woman too from perishing with her child, the doctors [attended] to operate on the baby and draw it out by cutting it limb by limb." While the procedure ultimately does not need to happen thanks to the miraculous workings of a relic, the author, without any moralization or shame, details here the contemporaneous procedures for an embryotomy, as described in medieval surgical manuals.

Further corroborating the continued use of this surgery, we can note that the sixth-century text by Aëtius of Amida (citing a certain Philumenos and Soranus), details the operation for an embryotomy similarly. The same operation is also recounted perfectly in Paul of Aegina's own seventh-century compendium on surgical practices.

These late-term abortions echo their modern counterpart, demonstrating that this was a known and established practice in the Middle Ages. This medical knowledge flourished in particular in the Greek-speaking, eastern Roman Empire, most commonly known to us today as the Byzantine Empire. Glimmers of the medical prowess of the Byzantine Empire and its long-thriving history are scattered across medieval sources.

In fact, one of the first recorded uses of a Caesarian section on a living woman comes down to us from Visigothic Spain, but the text tells us the deed was performed by a skilled "Greek" (aka Byzantine) doctor, who is called to save the life of a living mother whose child has died in the womb.

While Caesarians were used in antiquity, they were deployed then only to rescue a child from a dead mother. In the *Lives of the Fathers of Mérida*, composed in the 630s, the author chronicles the life of Paul, bishop of Mérida around 540/550. Paul is a Greek who had trained as a doctor in his youth. In order to save the life of a wealthy woman, he must put his clerical garments aside and sully his hands with an embryotomy. The text describes how "with wonderous skill he made a most skillful incision by his cunning use of a knife and extracted the already decaying body of the infant, limb by limb, piece by piece," in order to save the woman's life.

The only difference between the figure of the sex worker shamed for her abortions and the persons for whom these gynecological and surgical books were commissioned is that the latter were courtly elites. Therefore, they had better recourses to medical knowledge, treatment and privacy.

But, the fact that stories of late-term abortions even find their way into saints' lives without judgment belie a more important fact: that abortions undertaken for the preservation of a woman's life or health were rarely, if ever, under attack by medieval Christian authors. Not even the moralizing religious texts touch upon such cases. This is a fact that modern Christian pundits have not merely forgotten, but just never learned.

About the Author

Roland Betancourt is a professor of art history, Director of Visual Studies and a Chancellor's Fellow at the University of California, Irvine. He is the author of Byzantine Intersectionality: Sexuality, Gender, and Race in the Middle Ages *(Princeton University Press, 2020).*

The Forgotten History of the World's First Trans Clinic

By Brandy Schillace

Late one night on the cusp of the 20th century, Magnus Hirschfeld, a young doctor, found a soldier on the doorstep of his practice in Germany. Distraught and agitated, the man had come to confess himself an *Urning*–a word used to refer to homosexual men. It explained the cover of darkness; to speak of such things was dangerous business. The infamous "Paragraph 175" in the German criminal code made homosexuality illegal; a man so accused could be stripped of his ranks and titles and thrown in jail.

Hirschfeld understood the soldier's plight–he was himself both homosexual and Jewish–and did his best to comfort his patient. But the soldier had already made up his mind. It was the eve of his wedding, an event he could not face. Shortly after, he shot himself.

The soldier bequeathed his private papers to Hirschfeld, along with a letter: "The thought that you could contribute to [a future] when the German fatherland will think of us in more just terms," he wrote, "sweetens the hour of death." Hirschfeld would be forever haunted by this needless loss; the soldier had called himself a "curse," fit only to die, because the expectations of heterosexual norms, reinforced by marriage and law, made no room for his kind. These heartbreaking stories, Hirschfeld wrote in *The Sexual History of the World War*, "bring before us the whole tragedy [in Germany]; what fatherland did they have, and for what freedom were they fighting?" In the aftermath of this lonely death, Hirschfeld left his medical practice and began a crusade for justice that would alter the course of queer history.

Hirschfeld sought to specialize in sexual health, an area of growing interest. Many of his predecessors and colleagues believed that homosexuality was pathological, using new theories from psychology to suggest it was a sign of mental ill health. Hirschfeld, in contrast, argued that a person may be born with characteristics that did not fit into heterosexual or binary categories and supported the idea that a "third sex" (or *Geschlecht*) existed naturally. Hirschfeld proposed the term "sexual intermediaries" for nonconforming individuals. Included under this umbrella were what he considered "situational" and "constitutional" homosexuals–a recognition that there is often a spectrum of bisexual practice–as well as what he termed "transvestites." This group included those who wished to wear the clothes of the opposite sex and those who "from the point of view of their character" should be considered as the opposite sex. One soldier with whom Hirschfeld had worked described wearing women's clothing as the chance "to be a human being at least for a moment." He likewise recognized that these people could be either homosexual or heterosexual, something that is frequently misunderstood about transgender people today.

Perhaps even more surprising was Hirschfeld's inclusion of those with no fixed gender, akin to today's concept of gender-fluid or nonbinary identity (he counted French novelist George Sand among them). Most important for Hirschfeld, these people were acting "in accordance with their nature," not against it.

If this seems like extremely forward thinking for the time, it was. It was possibly even more forward than our own thinking, 100 years later. Current anti-trans sentiments center on the idea that being transgender is both new and unnatural. In the wake of a U.K. court decision in 2020 limiting trans rights, an editorial in the *Economist* argued that other countries should follow suit, and an editorial in the *Observer* praised the court for resisting a "disturbing trend" of children receiving gender-affirming health care as part of a transition.

But history bears witness to the plurality of gender and sexuality. Hirschfeld considered Socrates, Michelangelo and Shakespeare to be sexual intermediaries; he considered himself and his partner Karl Giese to be the same. Hirschfeld's own predecessor in sexology, Richard von Krafft-Ebing, had claimed in the 19th century that homosexuality was natural sexual variation and congenital.

Hirschfeld's study of sexual intermediaries was no trend or fad; instead it was a recognition that people may be born with a nature contrary to their assigned gender. And in cases where the desire to live as the opposite sex was strong, he thought science ought to provide a means of transition. He purchased a Berlin villa in early 1919 and opened the *Institut für Sexualwissenschaft* (the Institute for Sexual Research) on July 6. By 1930 it would perform the first modern gender-affirmation surgeries in the world.

A Place of Safety

A corner building with wings to either side, the institute was an architectural gem that blurred the line between professional and intimate living spaces. A journalist reported it could not be a scientific institute, because it was furnished, plush and "full of life everywhere." Its stated purpose was to be a place of "research, teaching, healing, and refuge" that could "free the individual from physical ailments, psychological afflictions, and social deprivation." Hirschfeld's institute would also be a place of education. While in medical school, he had experienced the trauma of watching as a gay man was paraded naked before the class, to be verbally abused as a degenerate.

Hirschfeld would instead provide sex education and health clinics, advice on contraception, and research on gender and sexuality, both anthropological and psychological. He worked tirelessly to try to overturn Paragraph 175. Unable to do so, he got legally accepted "transvestite" identity cards for his patients, intended to prevent them from being arrested for openly dressing and living as the opposite sex. The grounds also included room for offices given over to feminist activists, as well as a printing house for sex reform journals meant to dispel myths about sexuality. "Love," Hirschfeld said, "is as varied as people are."

The institute would ultimately house an immense library on sexuality, gathered over many years and including rare books and diagrams and protocols for male-to-female (MTF) surgical transition. In addition to psychiatrists for therapy, he had hired Ludwig Levy-

Lenz, a gynecologist. Together, with surgeon Erwin Gohrbandt, they performed male-to-female surgery called *Genitalumwandlung*–literally, "transformation of genitals." This occurred in stages: castration, penectomy and vaginoplasty. (The institute treated only trans women at this time; female-to-male phalloplasty would not be practiced until the late 1940s.) Patients would also be prescribed hormone therapy, allowing them to grow natural breasts and softer features.

Their groundbreaking studies, meticulously documented, drew international attention. Legal rights and recognition did not immediately follow, however. After surgery, some trans women had difficulty getting work to support themselves, and as a result, five were employed at the institute itself. In this way, Hirschfeld sought to provide a safe space for those whose altered bodies differed from the gender they were assigned at birth–including, at times, protection from the law.

Lives Worth Living

That such an institute existed as early as 1919, recognizing the plurality of gender identity and offering support, comes as a surprise to many. It should have been the bedrock on which to build a bolder future. But as the institute celebrated its first decade, the Nazi party was already on the rise. By 1932 it was the largest political party in Germany, growing its numbers through a nationalism that targeted the immigrant, the disabled and the "genetically unfit." Weakened by economic crisis and without a majority, the Weimar Republic collapsed.

Adolf Hitler was named chancellor on January 30, 1933, and enacted policies to rid Germany of *Lebensunwertes Leben*, or "lives unworthy of living." What began as a sterilization program ultimately led to the extermination of millions of Jews, Roma, Soviet and Polish citizens–and homosexuals and transgender people.

When the Nazis came for the institute on May 6, 1933, Hirschfeld was out of the country. Giese fled with what little he could. Troops swarmed the building, carrying off a bronze bust of Hirschfeld and all his precious books, which they piled in the street. Soon a towerlike bonfire engulfed more than 20,000 books, some of them rare copies that had helped provide a historiography for nonconforming people.

The carnage flickered over German newsreels. It was among the first and largest of the Nazi book burnings. Nazi youth, students and soldiers participated in the destruction, while voiceovers of the footage declared that the German state had committed "the intellectual garbage of the past" to the flames. The collection was irreplaceable.

Levy-Lenz, who like Hirschfeld was Jewish, fled Germany. But in a dark twist, his collaborator Gohrbandt, with whom he had performed supportive operations, joined the Luftwaffe as chief medical adviser and later contributed to grim experiments in the Dachau concentration camp. Hirschfeld's likeness would be reproduced on Nazi propaganda as the worst kind of offender (both Jewish and homosexual) to the perfect heteronormative Aryan race.

In the immediate aftermath of the Nazi raid, Giese joined Hirschfeld and his protégé Li Shiu Tong, a medical student, in Paris. The three would continue living together as partners and colleagues with hopes of rebuilding the institute, until the growing threat of Nazi occupation in Paris required them to flee to Nice. Hirschfeld died of a sudden stroke in 1935 while still on the run. Giese died by suicide in 1938. Tong abandoned his hopes of opening an institute in Hong Kong for a life of obscurity abroad.

Over time their stories have resurfaced in popular culture. In 2015, for instance, the institute was a major plot point in the second season of the television show *Transparent*, and one of Hirschfeld's patients, Lili Elbe, was the protagonist of the film *The Danish Girl*. Notably, the doctor's name never appears in the novel that inspired the movie, and despite these few exceptions the history of Hirschfeld's clinic has been effectively erased. So effectively, in fact, that although the Nazi newsreels still exist, and the pictures of the burning library are often reproduced, few know they feature the world's first trans clinic. Even that iconic image has been decontextualized, a nameless tragedy.

The Nazi ideal had been based on white, cishet (that is, cisgender and heterosexual) masculinity masquerading as genetic superiority.

Any who strayed were considered as depraved, immoral, and worthy of total eradication. What began as a project of "protecting" German youth and raising healthy families had become, under Hitler, a mechanism for genocide.

A Note for the Future

The future doesn't always guarantee progress, even as time moves forward, and the story of the Institute for Sexual Research sounds a warning for our present moment. Current legislation and indeed calls even to separate trans children from supportive parents bear a striking resemblance to those terrible campaigns against so-labeled aberrant lives.

Studies have shown that supportive hormone therapy, accessed at an early age, lowers rates of suicide among trans youth. But there are those who reject the evidence that trans identity is something you can be "born with." Evolutionary biologist Richard Dawkins was recently stripped of his "humanist of the year" award for comments comparing trans people to Rachel Dolezal, a civil rights activist who posed as a Black woman, as though gender transition were a kind of duplicity. His comments come on the heels of legislation in Florida aiming to ban trans athletes from participating in sports and an Arkansas bill denying trans children and teens supportive care.

Looking back on the story of Hirschfeld's institute–his protocols not only for surgery but for a trans-supportive community of care, for mental and physical healing, and for social change–it's hard not to imagine a history that might have been. What future might have been built from a platform where "sexual intermediaries" were indeed thought of in "more just terms"? Still, these pioneers and their heroic sacrifices help to deepen a sense of pride–and of legacy–for LGBTQ+ communities worldwide. As we confront oppressive legislation today, may we find hope in the history of the institute and a cautionary tale in the Nazis who were bent on erasing it.

The Disturbing History of Research into Transgender Identity

By Jack Turban

In 1975 psychiatrist Robert Stoller of the University of California, Los Angeles, wrote something bizarre in his textbook on sex and gender. He asserted that people who were assumed to be boys when they were born but whose gender identity or expression did not match that assumption "often have pretty faces, with fine hair, lovely complexions, graceful movements, and–especially–big, piercing, liquid eyes." Based on this observation, he suggested a theoretical model in which transgender girls become transgender because they are especially cute. Society treats them more like girls, he reasoned, and because of this experience, they start to identify as female.

As a physician-scientist, I'm generally of the opinion that knowledge leads to progress. But studies focused on this particular question–those asking what determines someone's gender identity–have led us down some strange and dangerous paths. Researchers in this area appear to be in search of some objective truth, but the science is rooted in a subjective assumption: that we need to know what makes someone transgender so that they can be "fixed." As a result, scientists have relentlessly pursued such questions, launching studies that promoted ideas that could hurt transgender children and their families.

Stoller's observations motivated many of the psychological theories behind what makes people transgender. In 1993 a group of researchers at the Clarke Institute of Psychiatry in Toronto set out to test his hypothesis that beauty and what was then called "gender identity disorder" were linked. They recruited 17 birth-assigned boys with the diagnosis and 17 birth-assigned boys without it, all around the age of eight. The researchers then took headshots of the children and showed them to 36 college students. The students were asked to rate the youngsters' physical appearance on a scale from one to five with categories such as "attractive," "handsome" and "beautiful." In the end, the college students found the children with "gender identity disorder" to be "prettier" than the cisgender boys. The findings seem to suggest Stoller was right: perhaps, because of their appearance, people treated the youngsters in the former group more like girls, and consequently, they became transgender. Though as the authors mention later in the paper, an equally plausible theory is that these children could have altered their appearance (long hair, et cetera) in ways that matched their identity, leading the college students to associate them with more feminine descriptions such as "pretty."

A few years later, researchers revived this line of investigation, using the headshots of young birth-assigned girls with "gender identity disorder." A group of college students again rated how "ugly" or "pretty" these children appeared, compared with cisgender girls. The children with "gender identity disorder" were rated as less beautiful, prompting the researchers to suggest that they may have been treated more like boys and thus identified as male. It seems more likely that these children simply cut their hair shorter, so the participants attached more masculine words to them. In the end, the study didn't reveal much about what makes someone transgender, but it did promote an offensive theory with the potential to diminish the self-esteem of vulnerable transgender youth.

Researchers also studied the parents of such children. Psychiatry has long been enamored with the theory of mothers harming the development of their children (for example, the refrigerator mother theory posited that autism was caused by a lack of maternal warmth). These studies similarly asked if perhaps parents were to "blame" for their kids' gender identity. In one paper, researchers assessed whether the mothers of children with "gender identity disorder" had more symptoms of either depression or a condition called borderline personality disorder. They found these mothers had more symptoms of both. Sounds convincing, right? Children must become transgender because their mothers are mentally ill.

What the researchers failed to discuss was that the mothers' symptoms could easily have been caused by the way society treated their children. The subscale of borderline personality disorder that was higher among them was "interpersonal conflict." You don't need to be the parent of a transgender child to imagine that raising your kid in an unaccepting community could create substantial conflict.

In another study, researchers noted that parents of children with "gender identity disorder" did not place strong limits on stereotypically gender atypical behaviors such as birth-assigned boys playing with dolls or birth-assigned girls playing with blocks or transportation toys. Perhaps this was the cause of the "problem"? If these parents had simply cracked down on this behavior early on–ripped the Barbie out of their toddler's hands, say–they may have prevented it, the authors posited. The more likely explanation is that it's difficult to take a doll away from a child who desperately wants to play with it. And that doing so makes them sad and impacts their self-esteem.

In each case, researchers were hyperfocused on finding a problem with either the kids or their parents. But in the end, these scientists failed to establish one. They seemed less interested in a vital reframing: perhaps the issue was not the children's identity but the way society treated them. Instead of supporting these kids, the researchers labeled them unattractive or painted their parents as mentally unstable.

These theories on the origins of gender identity have only added to the misguided, and increasingly illegal, calls for "therapies" designed to make transgender people cisgender. The logic of so-called gender identity conversion therapy is that if the environment is the cause, then we can simply alter the environment to nip things in the bud. Most of the "conversion" manuals have not been released to the public, but in 2002 a psychologist at Columbia University published "Gender Identity Disorder in Young Boys: A Parent and Peer-Based Protocol," which included parenting techniques such as "letting go of [the] boy by [the] mother," forcing the child to play with same-sex friends, and removing the youngster from stereotypically gender-atypical activities such as gymnastics or ballet. Notably, a recent study my colleagues and I conducted showed that attempts to change a child's gender identity from transgender to cisgender are associated with greater odds of attempting suicide. Several U.S.

states have banned conversion therapy, but in much of the U.S., these practices continue.

Similar research into the psychological causes of transgender identity continues even today. A physician at Brown University recently conducted an anonymous survey of respondents recruited via Web sites for parents who believe peer pressure and online influences have made their children transgender. The survey essentially asked the parents if they thought the Internet made their children trans, and the parents, not surprisingly, given that they were visiting Web sites about this idea, answered yes. Conservative media latched onto the study, suggesting that transgender children are really just confused kids tricked into being transgender after reading something on Reddit. The implication is that we need to take these kids away from supportive online LGBTQ communities so that they can be made cisgender again. Reading through this literature, we need to ask ourselves some questions: What is the reason for this research? What does it hope to accomplish? The tireless search reveals a thinly veiled dogma: that being transgender is a pathology to be fixed. This belief not only harms transgender people but also undermines good science.

What good science shows us is that when we accept transgender people, they thrive. Instead of trying to figure out what went "wrong," we should be investing our time and energy into advocating for nondiscrimination laws, increasing access to health care and raising transgender voices in the media, so society realizes that they are vital members of our communities. Maybe Stoller was right when he noted that those children were exceptional. It's time we celebrate that and move on.

About the Author

Jack Turban is a fellow in child and adolescent psychiatry at the Stanford University School of Medicine, where he researches the mental health of transgender youth. His writing has appeared in the New York Times, *the* Washington Post, *the* Los Angeles Times, *and more. Follow him on Twitter@jack_turban.*

Commentary: The Eugenics Legacy of the Nobelist Who Fathered IVF

By Osagie K. Obasogie

Robert G. Edwards might not be a household name, but the innovation he pioneered along with Patrick Steptoe certainly is. In vitro fertilization (IVF), the process whereby human eggs are fertilized outside of the body and the resulting embryos implanted in a woman's womb, led to the 1978 birth of Louise Brown–the world's first "test tube baby." To date, an estimated five million children worldwide have been born using this innovation. Edwards received the 2010 Nobel Prize in Physiology or Medicine for this remarkable achievement.

Edwards's passing earlier this year prompted an outpouring of praise. He has been widely described as a maverick researcher disinterested in personal recognition who simply wanted to give babies to those who couldn't make them on their own. The *New York Times* quoted Edwards's former collaborator, Barry Bavister, as saying "Dr. Edwards's motivation–his passion, in fact–was not fame or fortune but rather helping infertile women." Bavister continued, "He believed with all his heart that it was the right thing to do."

But Edwards's views on the technology he created and the uses to which it should be put may be more complicated than this portrayal. One detail omitted from the obituaries published around the world was that Edwards was a member in good standing of the Eugenics Society in Britain for much of his career. Recently uncovered documents show that Edwards served on the organization's Council–its leadership body–as a trustee on three separate occasions: from 1968 to 1970, 1971 to 1973 and once again from 1995 to 1997 after the group euphemistically renamed itself "The Galton Institute" for the founder of the eugenics movement, Francis Galton. As we consider Edwards's legacy in light of his recent passing, it is important to think critically about the relationship between Edwards's development of IVF and his participation in an organization that was dedicated to promoting one of the most dangerous ideas in human history: that science should be used to control human reproduction in order to breed preferred types of people.

Coined by Galton in the late 1800s to mean "well-born," eugenics became a dominant aspect of Western intellectual life and social policy during the first half of the 20th century. It started with the seemingly simple proposition that one's social position is rooted in heritable qualities of character and intellect.

Eugenicists of that era also believed that people with what they considered the least desirable traits tend to have the most children, precipitating what they saw as an inevitable decline in a society's intellectual and physical vigor. Taking their cue from livestock breeders, eugenicists argued that socially disadvantageous characteristics could be bred out of human populations through policies that limited the reproduction of "the unfit"–the "feebleminded," the poor and the weak. Many eugenicists considered these qualities to be more prevalent among racial and ethnic minorities.

Eugenics has had disturbing implications since its inception. Galton characterized it in 1883 as the "science of improving stock ... to give to the more suitable races or strains of blood a better chance of prevailing speedily over the less suitable than they otherwise would have had." Framed in this manner, eugenics has held an appeal to dictatorial and authoritarian regimes seeking to eradicate or discourage the growth of disfavored groups. The Nazis invoked eugenics to justify the extermination of people with disabilities, Jews, and other marginalized populations. And as a social philosophy eugenics also received approbation and financial support from the wealthy and other elites–particularly in the U.S. It was followed by the likes of philanthropists John D. Rockefeller and Nobel Prize–winning scientists such as William Shockley and Alexis Carrel. It even gained the support of women's health advocates such as Margaret Sanger.

Eugenics was duly stigmatized after World War II when the world saw the horrors of its most infamous implementation, the Holocaust. But many scientists continued to believe in its core tenet:

that social problems have fundamental biological underpinnings that can be eliminated through scientific control of human reproduction. Whereas prewar eugenics focused on "negative" applications–weeding out undesirables through practices such as forced sterilization and genocide–eugenicists in the postwar years emphasized so-called "positive eugenics," or strategically breeding in favorable traits. As early as the 1960s and continuing right up to the present, some scientists and others–including a number of well-respected scholars at prestigious institutions–have tried to resurrect eugenic projects in one guise or another. These enthusiasts promote the troubling idea that eugenic principles can be separated from the inequality, intolerance and oppression that gave rise to the movement in the late 19th century.

No one questions Edwards's clinical concern and goodwill in treating his patients, as documented by obituary writers. Yet he also seemed comfortable with placing IVF and other reproductive and genetic technologies in an intellectual framework that would have been eminently recognizable to Galton and his early disciples. Edwards believed that increased control over human reproduction could not only treat the infertile but also allow for socially favored characteristics to be selected and bred into the population. Edwards himself hinted at the link between IVF and eugenics when reflecting on the 25th anniversary of Louise Brown's birth in 1993, saying that developing IVF "was about more than infertility ... I wanted to find out exactly who was in charge, whether it was god himself or whether it was scientists in the laboratory." Edwards's conclusion?–"It was us."

Although there is nothing inherently eugenic about IVF, being able to manipulate human conception outside of the womb is an essential platform technology for any modern eugenic goal. Edwards implicitly acknowledged this link in 1999 when he said, "Soon it will be a sin of parents to have a child that carries the heavy burden of genetic disease. We are entering a world where we have to consider the quality of our children." The implications of this statement suggest not simply using new technologies to treat disease, but also to prevent the births or reconfigure the traits of individuals thought to be of low value.

But Edwards didn't stop there. He also supported the use of modern selection technologies for predetermining nonmedical traits that are viewed as more desirable in some societies, such as having a boy instead of a girl. Edwards's technology, IVF, combined with preimplantation genetic diagnosis–the ability to screen embryos for a particular trait before implanting them–are vitally important steps toward being able to select the features of future generations much like we currently configure the details for a new car. Edwards fully supported using sex selection technologies for social and not just medical reasons, saying: "Go ahead and use it. Those parents have to raise those children."

It is not simply that Edwards believed in the permissive implementation of reproductive and genetic technologies in a manner that happened to coincide with eugenic aspirations. Rather, he embraced eugenics as morally justifiable –save for the brief period when a presumably pure science was politicized by fanatics. Edwards said as much in 2004 during testimony before the Parliamentary Committee on Science and Technology in the British House of Commons. When asked whether a line could be drawn between new reproductive and genetic technologies and eugenics, Edwards–in a style reminiscent of former Pres. Bill Clinton–said, "It depends what we mean by eugenics." He continued, "Eugenics was started in the 1870s by an English geneticist who had the welfare of mankind in his mind. The work became degraded after 1930 caused by the Nazis ... [and] various other things where people were found not to be behaving themselves correctly. So, the word became degraded...."

Whereas Edwards noted that these technologies can go forward without using the specific term "eugenics," his statement is quite revealing if only for its stunning inaccuracy. No respectable historian of this period would characterize Galton's ambitions so charitably nor would any suggest that the Nazis were the first or only group to brutally implement eugenics as law and public policy. (The world's first eugenics law–providing for forced sterilizations–was passed in

Indiana in 1907. Many of these practices continued in other states until the 1970s.) Edwards's thinly veiled attempt at rehabilitating eugenics as not only a defensible concept but somehow as a social movement with a misunderstood history is deeply problematic.

Some try to distinguish (and therefore obscure and excuse) postwar eugenic advocates like Edwards from their prewar predecessors by focusing on the modern emphasis on individuals. By no means did Edwards or his contemporaries advocate the state-enforced eugenic policies of the 1920s and 1930s. They continue to believe in markets and choice; individuals should have access to technologies that allow them to control and enhance human traits. The new eugenicists hope that the market dynamics surrounding the availability of selection and enhancement technologies will mirror other consumer pressures–akin to upgrading to the newest iPhone–to elicit broad-based societal demand that facilitates the goal of population-wide improvements in the "quality" of the human genetic stock.

But this emphasis on individual choice as a distinguishing factor is illusory at best. Past state-enforced eugenics and the prospects for what some call a new free-market eugenics are connected by an incessant desire to link social problems to human biology rather than to political and economic conditions that underlie apparent disparities in abilities among different social groups. A troubling yet consistent theme for eugenics is that only certain types of people–the smart, the beautiful and those without disability–deserve to exist, as those who are less than ideal are simply too burdensome.

It is this notion that science can perfect the human condition and technology can solve social problems that leads otherwise intelligent and well-meaning people to adhere to eugenics's disastrous social policies and scientific projects. Despite attempts to rehabilitate the term, what connects old-school eugenics with the postwar and 21st-century versions is the hubris embedded in an underlying attitude that scientists and other elites should take control of evolution to predetermine–or redesign–humanity's biological landscape. Edwards articulated this perspective in 1974 when speculating on the possibility of cloning humans–a quintessentially eugenic pursuit that envisions replicating individuals with genetic endowments thought to be ideal. Although acknowledging possible limitations, he broadly stated that "any [scientific] method of potential value in raising human standards should be considered, and [human reproductive] cloning might contribute towards this end by providing pools of talent."

We can all celebrate the happiness that IVF has brought to many. And, with sufficient oversight of an increasingly sprawling and unregulated fertility industry, IVF need not lead to a parade of horribles. But as we consider the legacy of Robert G. Edwards we must put into perspective the views he held that bear clear links to ignoble attitudes and social policies: the breeding of humans to fit certain predefined specifications that conform to social norms that are all too easily biased. In that sense Edwards's eugenic aspirations should be part of his legacy. The arrogance and cruelty embedded in these beliefs should serve as a clear warning against revisiting a path that science and society should never again travel.

About the Author

Osagie K. Obasogie is Haas Distinguished Chair and a professor of bioethics at the University of California, Berkeley, in the Joint Medical Program and School of Public Health and is a Senior Fellow with the Center for Genetics and Society. He is author of "Blinded by Sight: Seeing Race through the Eyes of the Blind" (Stanford University Press, 2013) and co-editor of the forthcoming volume "Beyond Bioethics: Toward a New Biopolitics" (University of California Press, March 2018).

Section 7: Public Health

7.1 Immunization against Smallpox before Jenner
By William L. Langer

7.2 What Florence Nightingale Can Teach Us about Architecture and Health
By Steven Lockley

7.3 We Learned the Wrong Lessons from the Tuskegee 'Experiment'
By Melba Newsome

7.4 In the Fight against Infectious Disease, Social Changes Are the New Medicine
By Maryn McKenna

Immunization against Smallpox before Jenner

By William L. Langer

In the 17th century smallpox, a disease that is now on the verge of eradication, was endemic everywhere in Europe and probably throughout the world. Perhaps the most infectious disease of man, it was in many respects even more loathsome and fearful than that other great killer, plague. Where plague decided between life and death within three or four days, smallpox lasted for two weeks or longer. Its first signs were fever, backache and vomiting. The fever then subsided, and many small bumps the size of birdshot appeared on the skin, particularly on the face, the chest and the arms. Over several days the bumps enlarged as they filled with fluid. The fever then returned and the bumps became inflamed and swollen pustules that broke and formed a soft yellow crust with an offensive odor. Eventually, if the patient survived (and in many epidemics two in five died), the crusts fell off, revealing the characteristic pox, or depressed scars, that gave the disease its name. It was not unusual for the patient also to be left blind.

Although smallpox most commonly attacked children under five, it did not respect age or social status. Scarcely 20 percent of the population escaped it entirely, and it was always more virulent in the cities than it was in the countryside. In 17th-century London it accounted for some 10 percent of all deaths, and it took an even higher toll in other European cities. Like plague it would assume epidemic proportions every five to 10 years. About 1660, just as plague was beginning to die out in Europe, the threat from smallpox increased. Not long afterward the intelligentsia of Europe awakened to a fact already known to common folk: this terrifying scourge was avoidable. Smallpox was in fact the first major disease that was amenable to a form of prophylaxis; it could not be cured but it could be prevented.

Today the prevention of smallpox is usually associated with the name of Edward Jenner. Actually people in many parts of the Old World had practiced one method or another of "buying the pox" long before Jenner's time. Fearful for their children's health, parents would seek out someone with a case of smallpox, preferably a mild one. The smallpox victim and the child would then make contact in such a way as to infect the child. After an incubation period of about a week the child, if he was lucky, would develop a mild case of smallpox and would emerge virtually unscarred and immune to the disease thereafter; the mild induced case gave the same protection that was provided by a severe one. Educated people came to call this practice of folk medicine inoculation, after the Latin inoculare, to graft. They also called it variolation; variola, from the Latin varus, pimple, was the scholarly name for smallpox.

There were numerous techniques of variolation. The Chinese avoided direct contact with the sick; instead the child was induced to inhale a powder made from the crusts shed by a recovering patient. In the Near East and in Africa fresh material from a diseased patient's pustules was rubbed into a cut or scratch in the skin of the person being immunized. The first scholarly account of peasant immunization practices in Europe appears to be one written by Thomas Bartholin, an anatomist at the University of Copenhagen and later physician to Christian V, king of Denmark and Norway; his note on variolation in the Danish countryside was published in 1675. At that time the practice was also known in rural France and in Wales.

In England 40 more years passed before the folk practices came to the notice of the learned. An Oxford-trained Greek physician then living in Constantinople, Emanuel Timoni, was the reporter. He wrote to the Royal Society of London in 1713 to describe to his fellow members the method of variolation used in the Near East. His note was summarized in the society's *Philosophical Transactions* in 1714. Two years later the same journal published a more detailed analysis of the Eastern practice written by an Italian physician, James Pylarini, who was then serving as the British consul in Smyrna. Variolation was practiced in Smyrna along well-established Near

Eastern lines; professional variolators, usually women, took material from a ripe pustule and rubbed it into a scratch or an incision in the arm or leg of the person being inoculated.

We now come to Mary Pierrepont, a well-born English beauty who against her father's wishes eloped in 1712 with Edward Wortley Montagu, a grandson of the first earl of Sandwich. The couple lived quietly in the country until Edward became a member of Parliament for Westminster in 1715 and his wife suddenly found herself one of the most popular hostesses in London and a friend of the leading intellectuals of the capital. That same year Lady Mary contracted smallpox, to the ruin of her beauty. The following year her husband was sent as ambassador to the Turkish court in Constantinople. Lady Mary, who now had an understandable interest in smallpox, was greatly impressed by what she saw of the Turkish practice of variolation. She had the embassy physician inoculate her young son, and on her return to London in 1718 she agitated enthusiastically in favor of variolation. When her daughter reached the age of four in 1721, Lady Mary made sure that she too was inoculated against smallpox. Although she was not the first to report the Eastern practice to the English, Lady Mary deserves great credit both for her courage in having her children inoculated and for her persistent propaganda in court circles.

Lady Mary and those physicians who, having read the Royal Society reports, also favored the practice met with sustained and not entirely irrational opposition. Many clergymen simply denounced variolation as an interference with God's will. The fact remains that a few of those who were inoculated did die. More important, all who were inoculated became potential sources of contagion throughout the period of their illness.

Curiously, this contagious effect had not been foreseen and might have continued to go unnoticed except for an incident in the country north of London. The physician who had variolated Lady Mary's son in Constantinople had by now returned to England and happened to variolate the daughter of a Hertford Quaker. The household staff was large, and in the course of the little girl's illness and convalescence six of the servants (who had never contracted smallpox and therefore had no immunity) came in close contact with the child. All six were stricken, and a local epidemic ensued. Thus although a certain degree of progress was achieved (George I, for example, allowed the royal grandchildren to be immunized), variolation in England remained the exception rather than the rule.

At the same time inoculation against smallpox was initiated quite independently on the other side of the Atlantic. Boston was then the intellectual center of the British colonies in America, and Cotton Mather, the eminent theologian and far-ranging scholar, was a member of the Royal Society of London. Mather read the society's *Philosophical Transactions*, and soon after the appearance of Timoni's note he wrote a friend in England to say that one of his slaves had already told him of variolation as it was practiced in Africa.

In April, 1721, a smallpox epidemic broke out in Boston. Mather tried to mobilize the physicians of the city for a campaign of immunization. With one exception the response was outspokenly negative. The exception was Zabdiel Boylston. On June 26 Boylston inoculated his six-year-old son, one of his slaves and the slave's three-year-old boy, all without any adverse effects. Boylston thereupon proceeded to inoculate more than 200 other Bostonians in spite of a vigorous newspaper and pamphlet campaign in opposition to the practice. Unlike the opposition in England, Boylston's principal adversaries were his fellow physicians. The clergy on the whole supported Mather and Boylston.

The issue was a grave one, because the 1721 epidemic was unusually severe. Almost half of the population of Boston, 5,889 of the city's 12,000 inhabitants (11,720 if one subtracts the 280 immunized by Boylston and two other physicians), contracted smallpox. Of this number 844, or every seventh victim, died. The next smallpox epidemic to strike Boston, a less severe outbreak in 1730, was met with a much more widespread inoculation program.

Meanwhile in England interest in variolation continued to decline until John Kirkpatrick, an American physician from Charleston, S.C., visited London in 1743. He brought to English medical circles details of how inoculation had successfully halted a particularly severe outbreak of smallpox in Charleston in 1738. Kirkpatrick gave credit to an improved method of variolation that had reduced the severity of the disease in inoculated patients and had lowered the mortality rate among the immunized to one in 100. (About one in 50 of Boylston's patients had died.)

Kirkpatrick's report reopened the debate over inoculation in England. In 1746 a special facility, the Smallpox and Inoculation Hospital, was founded in London with the patronage of the duke of Marlborough. Although the hospital's capacity was limited, it quickly became a center of study and teaching; many students from abroad went there to learn the techniques of variolation. In 1754 Kirkpatrick's account of the success in Charleston was published. Translated into French and other languages, it soon became virtually a catechism. The next year Robert and Daniel Sutton, father and son, began to practice variolation, first in Suffolk and then in London. The Suttons made many improvements in variolation technique, and before moving to London they reported that they had inoculated 2,514 individuals without a single fatality. Daniel opened a private clinic in the city and soon attracted an imposing clientele of well-to-do Londoners. It is reported that he earned 2,000 guineas in 1764 and 6,500 the following year.

There is nothing implausible in Sutton's financial success; by the middle of the 18th century, as one authority notes, variolation had become a "social institution." Several dozen young physicians, having learned the technique of variolation, set up practice on the Continent and made a good living; the situation was much as it is today, when golf clubs on the Continent think that in order to gain prestige they must have a Scottish professional. The clientele, however, continued to be drawn mainly from the upper classes. For example, in 1756 a Geneva physician, Theodore Tronchin, was summoned to Paris to inoculate the family of the Duc d'Orléans, second in rank only to the king. So great was the excitement that elegant carriages formed a queue at Tronchin's door, much as if their owners were attending a performance at the Comédie Française.

In spite of exceptions such as this one, inoculation in Europe remained virtually an English monopoly. When professional inoculators were called in to train a corps of local physicians in the techniques of variolation (for example, a team was called to Potsdam by Frederick the Great and another to Vienna by the Empress Maria Theresa), it was from England that they were summoned. The French did not begin to catch up with the English in this respect until the mid-1750's, after another smallpox epidemic had broken out. With some interruptions the outbreak continued until the 1790's, and during those years the disease attacked a larger percentage of adults than usual.

Voltaire, who had survived an attack of smallpox at the age of 29, was a staunch advocate of inoculation. The prime mover among the French, however, was not Voltaire but a scientist of great eminence, Charles Marie de La Condamine, a mathematician and geographer whose fame sprang from an expedition to the Amazon in the 1730's. La Condamine went into action during the epidemic of the 1750's. In 1754 he published a number of tracts attacking the clergy's will-of-God position (an argument that appears to have been particularly influential in France) and advocated variolation as a means of controlling the epidemic. The Parlement of Paris, the chief judicial body of France, reacted to popular pressure by appointing a commission of 12 from the Faculty of Medicine of the University of Paris to investigate the issue and draft a report.

After much argument the commission split evenly for and against variolation, but when at last it reported the stalemate, the Faculty of Medicine as a whole had already come to favor this means of preventing smallpox. The practice was sanctioned by the Parlement until in 1763 a fresh epidemic in the city (urban areas were always the worst hit) was attributed to the contagion that inevitably accompanied inoculation. The Parlement responded by forbidding variolation within the Paris city limits, but the inoculators reacted to the prohibition by opening clinics just outside the capital. Among those practitioners, in addition to various English professionals and Tronchin, was a Venetian physician, Angelo Gatti, who lived in Paris and contributed substantially to the study of the disease. Five years later the Parlement rescinded its prohibition.

A roster of the better-known victims of the mid-century epidemics dramatizes the fact that smallpox did not respect the rich and powerful. In 1759 the most notable victim was the empress of Austria, Maria Theresa, stricken at the age of 52. She recovered and later engaged a Dutch physician to inoculate the members of the imperial family. In 1774 the most notable victim was the king of France, Louis XV, stricken at 64. After two weeks of agony he died; his malodorous body was hurried to the grave at night for fear that in those troubled times the usual pomp of a royal funeral might provoke a popular uprising. His death so frightened his successor, Louis XVI, that the monarch immediately had the entire royal family inoculated.

Perhaps inspired by Maria Theresa's experience or perhaps because of the hideous appearance of her own pockmarked late husband, Czar Peter, Catherine the Great summoned a London physician, Thomas Dimsdale, to St. Petersburg in 1768 to inoculate her and her son and heir, the Grand Duke Paul. This Dimsdale did without mishap in the fall of 1768. The grateful Catherine not only bestowed the title of baron on Dimsdale but also gave him a cash gift of 10,000 pounds (and another 2,000 pounds to cover expenses) and established an annuity of 500 pounds for him. This must surely be the highest compensation paid by anyone in exchange for immunity against smallpox. In 1781 Dimsdale made a second journey to Russia to inoculate Catherine's grandsons, Constantine and Alexander. During that visit he also immunized many other members of the Russian aristocracy, both in St. Petersburg and in Moscow.

By the eve of the French Revolution the method of inoculation had been so improved that a small pinprick and a drop of thin pus inserted by lancet served the purpose. It would probably be safe to say that everywhere in Europe a majority of the well-to-do had been variolated; after all, it was an excellent investment for those who could afford it. Some students of 18th-century population growth have suggested that the widespread practice had noticeably reduced the overall mortality rate in Europe and was thus responsible, at least in part, for the phenomenal increase in population at that time. There can be no certain judgment on the point; it is impossible, first, to establish the death rate for a time before the initiation of the census and, second, to speak with any assurance of the extent of successful immunization. The suggestion does, however, raise a further question: To what extent was variolation practiced among urban and rural workers? The urban poor in particular were the traditional incubators of endemic disease, and they made up the vast majority of the population in all cities. If they were not inoculated, there could be no hope of eradicating smallpox.

The well-to-do were not blind to the problem. Public clinics were opened and in some instances offered free inoculation for children. In England, Jonas Hanway, a well-known philanthropist and a trustee of the Foundling Hospital, suggested to his peers that they employ no servants who had not had smallpox or been inoculated against it. The younger Sutton, whose clinic was perhaps the most elegant in London, offered to variolate 400 children, 100 at a time, and care for them for a full month afterward if rich patrons would subscribe a guinea per head. Nothing came of his proposition, presumably for lack of subscribers.

As for the urban poor themselves, they seem to have shown no great interest in the issue. Naturally suspicious of approaches by their social superiors, they may also have held the pessimistic view that smallpox was an integral part of life. Perhaps they had no reason to think otherwise. Those of them who favored variolation would have looked to itinerant inoculators or even to amateurs for treatment. Such practitioners could not have been relied on to do an up-to-date job. More important, it would have been impossible in the urban slums to isolate the newly inoculated. Inoculated children would not have felt the effects for a week or so and would have continued to be in contact with others. It is reasonable to suppose they would thus have infected other children, who would then have come down with a full-blown case of the disease. If new contagion of this kind was commonplace, it is not hard to understand why many believed smallpox was constantly gaining ground. Contemporary writings contain eloquent testimony to a veritable panic over the disease that seized all Europe in the last quarter of the 18th century.

Much later, in 1852, Thackeray, recalling his life early in the 19th century, noted that at that time hundreds died or rose from their sickbed terribly scarred and disfigured. "In my early days," he wrote in *Henry Esmond*, "this pestilence would enter a village and destroy half the inhabitants: at its approach, it may well be imagined, not only the beautiful but the strongest were alarmed and those fled who could." There is more than enough contemporary evidence to show that Thackeray's remarks were not exaggerated.

Under the circumstances many physicians sought ways to prevent the infection that resulted from variolation. Jenner, a physician with a preference for a country practice, noted in the 1790s that the dairymaids in his neighborhood rarely, if ever, contracted smallpox, even in the absence of inoculation. After years of careful observation and experiment he published in 1798 a 70-page pamphlet: "An Inquiry into the Causes and Effects of the *Variolae Vaccinae*." (*Variolae vaccinae* was cowpox, the bovine form of smallpox.) In this classic report Jenner advanced the notion that inoculation with cowpox, which he considered a mild form of smallpox, would provide the same immunity to smallpox that variolation did. What was more important, the disease produced by vaccination, as opposed to variolation, would be so extremely mild that the vaccinated individual would not be a source of infection.

No better news could have reached the world in the midst of the Napoleonic Wars. Jenner's thesis was accepted at once by the great majority of physicians, and within a year or two thousands had been vaccinated. The news raced around the world faster than news had ever traveled before; Jenner was hailed everywhere as mankind's greatest benefactor, and his discovery was characterized as the most important medical advance of all time.

It is not my purpose here even to touch on the history of vaccination in the 19th and 20th centuries except to note that for all its benefits the procedure was not quite as simple and the immunity it conferred was not as long-lived as Jenner and the early vaccinators had supposed. Nonetheless, it seems appropriate to close this review of the antecedents of Jenner's great discovery with a note on its instant adoption in the U.S.

At the close of the 18th century a highly imaginative (although somewhat eccentric and testy) Harvard professor of medicine, Benjamin Waterhouse, played a role not unlike the one played by Mather and Boylston in the opening decades of the century. Waterhouse had been educated in Europe and maintained a regular correspondence with his friends there. Having received a copy of Jenner's pamphlet almost as soon as it could arrive by ship, Waterhouse was at once converted to Jenner's view. He wrote to friends in England asking for some of the cowpox material used for vaccination. It arrived in July, 1800, and he immediately vaccinated his children and servants.

Waterhouse promptly notified Thomas Jefferson, who was then vice-president, of Jenner's discovery. That always inquisitive statesman at once sought Waterhouse's good offices in securing an ample supply of the vaccine. Jefferson and his son thereupon vaccinated their entire household of 60, slaves included. As president, Jefferson went on to use his influence to establish the new procedure in Philadelphia and the other cities of the young republic. Before Jefferson's retirement to Monticello in 1809 the number of people who had been vaccinated on both sides of the Atlantic could be reckoned in the millions. The campaign to eradicate smallpox, now coming to a close after nearly two centuries, had begun in earnest.

What Florence Nightingale Can Teach Us about Architecture and Health

By Steven Lockley

In the late 19th century, Florence Nightingale revolutionized hospital design in what became known as Nightingale wards. The signature innovation of these wards was large windows that allowed cross-ventilation and abundant natural light. Nightingale believed that the light and air quality in a hospital's environment play an important role in speeding patient recovery. In the decades since, numerous studies have shown that Nightingale was right: daylight is a critical determinant of human health and wellness. Patients in rooms with daylight and views of the outdoors have quicker recovery times and need fewer painkillers. Natural light has been shown to decrease heart rate, lower blood pressure, and even treat depression faster than antidepressants. Importantly, just as Nightingale theorized, daylight can also decrease harmful bacteria and viruses.

Our understanding of how these benefits of light are delivered has advanced dramatically in the past two decades. Up until the end of the last century, it was assumed that all responses to ocular light exposure were mediated by the rods and cones we use to see, located at the back of the retinae. About 20 years ago, however, that assumption was completely transformed when research from many laboratories culminated in the discovery of light-sensitive cells in the ganglion layer at the front of the retinae that can function separately from the visual system.

These cells, dubbed "nonvisual photoreceptors," play an important role in maintaining our sleep, productivity and overall health. The cells are particularly sensitive to the short-wavelength blue light corresponding closely to peak wavelengths found in sunlight. Exposure to this short-wavelength light stimulates us, keeping us alert, improving reaction times, learning and a range of other cognitive functions. Light, particularly short-wavelength light, also elevates mood, and, in clinical patients, can be used treat depressive disorders and fatigue. Many artificial light sources emit a greater proportion of longer-wavelength light, however, which can undermine the benefits of daylight when indoors.

These nonvisual cells are also the primary timekeeper for our biological clocks–our circadian rhythms–located in the suprachiasmatic nuclei, a region of the hypothalamus in the brain. The circadian system regulates many of our bodily functions, including hormone levels, body temperature and metabolism, among many others. We take this synchronizing effect of light for granted. People who are totally blind–whose eyes cannot detect light–develop a debilitating condition called non-24-hour sleep-wake rhythm disorder, where their biological clocks run in and out of sync with the 24-hour day in a never-ending cycle. We experience a similar but temporary disconnection from the light-dark cycle when we work night shifts or travel quickly across time zones (jet lag).

In no part of our lives does this disconnect manifest itself more clearly than our sleep, as the circadian system strongly influences the timing and quality of sleep. A recent NIH-funded study found that nearly a third of Americans sleep six hours or less each night. According to the Centers for Disease Control and Prevention, sleep disorders are so common in the United States, they now constitute a public health epidemic. Lack of sleep is associated with many chronic health conditions, including heart disease, diabetes, depression and even some forms of cancer. Productivity losses due to poor sleep cost the economy billions of dollars every year. Exposure to a more robust light-dark cycle will help maintain better circadian synchronization and sleep, while greater daytime light exposure will also improve alertness and performance through its direct stimulant properties. In one recent study, office workers provided with increased daylight exposure slept 37 minutes longer compared to when they worked in a similar office with blinds, and exhibited 42 percent higher scores on a cognitive test taken at the end of the workday.

There are a number of ways to improve our access to daylight and improve our health in the process. In an office setting, architectural design can introduce more daylight deeper into buildings through larger windows and low desk partitions. Innovations such as smart glass make it possible to control the amount of daylight that enters through a window by automatically tinting based on cloud cover and the angle of the sun, eliminating the need for blinds and shades, allowing for views of the outdoors. Unlike opt-in employee wellness programs that require people to change their behavior, like gyms, natural light in the office provides wellness in a passive manner, benefiting all occupations equally. In places that are unable to provide ample natural light, workplaces should install daylight-mimicking LED lights with a spectrum peaking in the short-wavelength blue range.

During the COVID-19 pandemic, the same strategies should be applied to our home offices. We can promote our personal sleep quality and daytime productivity by working near a window or outside. In the evening, we can reduce our exposure to light by using dimmer lights, choosing blue-depleted warmer-looking lights, and minimizing use of light-emitting electronic devices for as long as possible before bed.

The benefits of regular exposure to daylight are clear and relatively easy to achieve. Yet, such innovations are implemented too rarely. While building developers and owners may not receive the direct benefit of better lighting, their tenants will, and providing a better environment may differentiate them from their competitors. Tenants, while often unable to design their own spaces, can include daylight access as a deciding factor in selecting real estate so that they reap the benefits of the greater productivity brought about by better lighting design. Bright days and dark nights support the body's circadian functions, enhance alertness and improve productivity. Simply put, greater access to daylight is the first simple step to better health. Nightingale grasped this more than a century ago. It's time to put her advice to work.

About the Author

Steven Lockley is an associate professor of medicine at Harvard Medical School who studies circadian rhythms and sleep.

We Learned the Wrong Lessons from the Tuskegee 'Experiment'

By Melba Newsome

Rarely a day goes by without national news stories about vaccine hesitancy: how many people say they definitely will or won't get a shot and how many are in the "maybe" box. No account is complete without a particular focus on Black people who–despite contracting, being made severely ill by and dying from coronavirus at elevated rates–express a high degree of reluctance to being injected with something developed to save their lives.

When asked to explain why so many Black people simply don't trust the federal government with their health, a common answer is "because of what happened at Tuskegee." Reference to that seminal event has become shorthand for past medical betrayal, abuse and exploitation at the highest levels.

Beginning in 1932, the U.S. Public Health Service dangled the promise of free medical care to recruit rural Black men in Alabama's Macon County to participate in the "Tuskegee Study of Untreated Syphilis in the Negro Male." Even after penicillin became widely available as an effective treatment 15 years later, the researchers withheld the drug and watched as the men died or were ravaged by the effects of untreated syphilis.

Based on my reporting and personal conversations with friends and family, it's clear many people don't know what happened at Tuskegee. They mistakenly believe the 600 Black men were injected with something bad (syphilis) that made them sick when, in reality, the 399 men who had the disease were denied something good (a dose of penicillin) that would have healed them.

Even many who have the details right learned the wrong lesson from that shameful episode in American medical history. Instead of rejecting vaccines and new therapeutics that are routinely used to successfully treat and cure a majority of the population, Tuskegee should have taught Black people to make a simple demand: give me whatever you're giving the white folk.

If that had happened 70 years ago, Tuskegee, Ala., might be better known for the historically Black university that bears its name than for a government injustice chronicled in books, movies, plays and congressional hearings.

My home state of North Carolina was one of the first to release coronavirus data by race. The numbers from Charlotte and Mecklenburg County showed the virus's disparate impact on people of color and were soon confirmed by the skyrocketing COVID-19 rates in other cities with high Black populations.

I saw early on how our well-justified mistrust of public health initiatives, a penchant for baseless conspiracy theories and a misreading of medical history would allow the crisis to take an outsize toll on the Black community.

That's why months later I decided to participate in the vaccine trials. I wanted to ensure that Black people were adequately represented in the research and to show that the vaccine should be embraced, not shunned. My motives weren't completely altruistic: clinical trial volunteers were supposed to be at or near the front of the line when a vaccine became available. That couldn't happen soon enough for me.

While some people thanked me for doing my part for medical science, others were perplexed and even angry that I would become a human guinea pig for the very medical establishment that has used our bodies for experimentation without care or consent.

The data and recent studies show that, rather than being recruited as lab rats, people of color are too often cut out of cutting-edge research. Black people make up about 14 percent of the U.S. population but, on average, only 5 percent of clinical trial participants for disease treatment.

It's almost taken as a given that our distrust is responsible for the low participation rates. But a study published in the journal *Cancer* found that some study recruiters viewed racial and ethnic minorities as less promising participants and in some cases reported withholding trial opportunities from them based on these perceptions.

That seemed to play out in the first phase I Moderna trial of 45 people; 40 were white, and two were Black. Pfizer and Moderna said diversity was a priority for their phase III trials to help ensure the vaccines' safety and effectiveness across populations and possibly reduce vaccine hesitancy; however, underrepresentation of Black people and other groups remained a concern.

My own experience suggests that their recruitment efforts could be improved. Last summer I started applying to participate in the clinical vaccine trials whenever I saw a call for volunteers. It took four applications and more than three months before I was at last selected for the Johnson & Johnson trial in mid-November.

Racism and discrimination in the health-care system show up in the form of neglect, indifference and dismissal. The COVID death toll was higher among Black and brown people because too many had their symptoms dismissed, were turned away from hospitals rather than admitted or were forced to work in dangerous conditions because they were deemed essential.

Much of the fear of the vaccine is prefaced on the assumption that Black people would be expected to go first to make sure it was safe for everybody else. The low numbers of people being vaccinated in the communities hardest hit by COVID-19 show that just the opposite has happened.

About the Author

Melba Newsome is a 2023 Alicia Patterson fellow, reporting on climate displacement and people of color.

In the Fight against Infectious Disease, Social Changes Are the New Medicine

By Maryn McKenna

In 1972 the distinguished virologist Frank Macfarlane Burnet looked back over medical progress made in the 20th century with considerable satisfaction, surveying it for the fourth edition of the book *Natural History of Infectious Disease*. That very year routine vaccination against smallpox had ceased in the U.S., no longer needed because the disease had been eliminated from the country. During the previous year the combined vaccine against measles, mumps and rubella had been licensed, and four years before, in 1968, a pandemic of influenza had been quelled by a new vaccine formula.

In 1960 Albert Sabin had delivered an oral vaccine against polio, and five years before that Jonas Salk had produced the first polio shot, preventing the dreaded paralysis that crippled children every summer. Since the time of World War II, drug development had delivered 12 separate classes of antibiotics, beginning with natural penicillin and ending seemingly forever the threat of deadly infections from childhood diseases, injuries, medical procedures and childbirth.

A few pages from the end of his book (co-authored with David O. White), Burnet made a bold prediction: "The most likely forecast about the future of infectious disease," he wrote, "is that it will be very dull."

Burnet was an experienced scientist who had shared the Nobel Prize in Physiology or Medicine in 1960 for pioneering ideas about the way people developed immune reactions. And at 73 he had lived through devastating epidemics, including the planet-spanning flu pandemic of 1918 while he was a university student in Australia. So he had seen a lot of advances and had played a role in some of them. "From the beginnings of agriculture and urbanization till well into the present century infectious disease was the major overall cause of human mortality," he wrote on the book's first page. "Now the whole pattern of human ecology has, temporarily at least, been changed."

Four years after Burnet made his optimistic prediction, the headmaster of a village school in what is now the Democratic Republic of the Congo collapsed with an unexplained bleeding disorder and died, the first recognized victim of Ebola virus. Nine years after his forecast, in 1981, physicians in Los Angeles and an epidemiologist at the U.S. Centers for Disease Control and Prevention diagnosed five young men in Los Angeles with an opportunistic pneumonia, the first signal of the worldwide pandemic of HIV/AIDS. In 1988 the gut bacterium *Enterococcus*, a common source of hospital infections, developed resistance to the last-resort antibiotic vancomycin, turning into a virulent superbug. And in 1997 a strain of influenza designated H5N1 jumped from chickens to humans in a market in Hong Kong, killing one third of the people it infected and igniting the first of multiple global waves of avian flu.

Those epidemics represent only a few of the infectious disease eruptions that now occur among humans every year, and efforts to stem them have taken on a renewed and urgent role in modern medicine. Some of these contagions are new to our species; others are resurgent old enemies. Sometimes their arrival sparks small outbreaks, such as an eruption of H7N7 avian flu in 2003 among 86 poultry-farm workers in the Netherlands. Now COVID-19, never before seen, has caused a global pandemic that has killed millions and sickened hundreds of millions.

None of these scenarios matches what Burnet envisioned. He thought of our engagement with infectious diseases simply as one mountain that we could climb and conquer. It might be more accurate to understand our struggle with microbes as a voyage across a choppy sea. At times we crest the waves successfully. In other moments, as in the COVID pandemic, they threaten to sink us.

It is difficult, under the weight of the novel coronavirus, to look far enough back in American history to perceive that–surprisingly–freedom from infectious disease was a part of the early New England colonists' experience. Beginning in the 1600s, these people fled

English and European towns drenched in sewage and riven with epidemics where they might be lucky to live to their 40th birthday. They found themselves in a place that felt blessed by God or good fortune where a man–or a woman who survived childbearing–could, remarkably, double that life span.

This was true, of course, only for the colonizers and not for the Indigenous Americans whom they displaced. The Spanish who arrived in Central and South America about a century earlier, and other European colonists who followed to the North, brought diseases so devastating to the precontact population that researchers have estimated 90 percent of the existing inhabitants were killed. Nor was it true for enslaved people brought to American shores, whose lives were cut short by abuse in the South's plantation system.

New Englanders before the 19th century, however, "had a very strange and unusual experience with infectious diseases," says David K. Rosner, a historian and co-director of the Center for the History and Ethics of Public Health at Columbia University. "When infections hit, and they did hit–smallpox, yellow fever–they were largely very localized and of relatively short duration."

At the time and through the early 1800s, disease was understood as a sign of moral transgression, a visitation meant to guide an erring population back to righteousness. In 1832 the edge of a worldwide pandemic of cholera washed up on the East Coast of the U.S., carried into port cities by ships plying trade routes. The governors of a dozen states declared a mandatory day of prayer and fasting. In New York the well-off fled the city for the socially distanced countryside, blaming the poor left behind for their own misfortune. A letter preserved by the New-York Historical Society, written by its founder, captures the callousness of some wealthy people: "Those sickened ... being chiefly of the very scum of the city, the quicker [their] dispatch the sooner the malady will cease."

Cholera was a global devastation, but it was also a doorway to our modern understanding of disease. Dogma held that its source was miasmas, bad air rising from rotting garbage and stagnant water. As late as 1874–20 years after physician John Snow traced the source of a London cholera outbreak to a neighborhood's well and halted it by removing the pump handle–an international conference on the disease declared that "the ambient air is the principal vehicle of the generative agent of cholera." It was not until 10 years later, when bacteriologist Robert Koch found identical bacteria in the feces of multiple cholera victims in India and reproduced the bacterium in a culture medium, that a microbe was proved to be the cause. (Koch was not aware that Italian bacteriologist Filippo Pacini had made the same observations in the year when Snow took the handle off the pump.)

This explanation for the source of cholera became one of the foundations of germ theory. The concept that disease could be transmitted and that the agents of transmission could be identified–and possibly blocked–transformed medicine and public health. The idea ignited a burst of innovation and civic commitment, a drive to clean up the cities whose filthy byways allowed disease-causing microbes to fester. Towns and states established municipal health departments and bureaus of sanitation, built sewer systems and long-distance water supplies, regulated food safety and ordered housing reform.

These improvements tipped industrial nations toward what would later be called the epidemiological transition, a concept coined by Abdel Omran in 1971 to describe the moment when deadly infections would retreat and slow-growing chronic diseases could become society's priority. Science started a seemingly unstoppable climb up the mountain of 20th-century achievement: viral identification, vaccine refinement, the development of antibiotics, the introduction of immunotherapies, the parsing of the human genome. Life expectancy in the U.S. rose from an average of 47 years in 1900 to 76 years toward the end of the century. The last case of smallpox, the only human disease ever eradicated, was recorded in 1978. The Pan American Health Organization declared its intention to eliminate polio from the Americas in 1985. The future seemed secure.

It was not, of course. In October 1988, in this magazine, Robert Gallo and Luc Montagnier (he died in 2022) wrote: "As recently as a decade ago it was widely believed that infectious disease was no longer much of a threat in the developed world.

The remaining challenges to public health there, it was thought, stemmed from noninfectious conditions such as cancer, heart disease and degenerative diseases. That confidence was shattered in the early 1980's by the advent of AIDS."

Gallo and Montagnier were co-discoverers of the HIV virus, working on separate teams in different countries. When they wrote their article, there had been more than 77,000 known cases of AIDS on the planet. (As of 2023, approximately 86 million people had been infected since the start of the epidemic.) As the researchers noted, recognition of the new illness punctured the sense of soaring assurance that infectious diseases had been conquered. Four years after Gallo and Montagnier wrote, 19 eminent scientists gathered by the Institute of Medicine (now part of the National Academies of Sciences, Engineering and Medicine) broadened the point in a sober book-length assessment of what they termed "emerging infections." Scientists and politicians had become complacent, they said, confident in the protection offered by antibiotics and vaccines and inattentive to the communicable disease threats posed by population growth, climate warming, rapid international travel, and the destruction of wild lands for settlements and mega-farms.

"There is nowhere in the world from which we are remote," the group warned, "and no one from whom we are disconnected." The scientists advocated urgent improvements in disease detection and reporting, data sharing, lab capacity, antibiotics and vaccines. Without those investments, they said, the planet would be perpetually behind when new diseases leaped into humans and catastrophically late in applying cures or preventions to keep them from spreading.

Their warning was prescient. At the time of their writing, the U.S. was recovering from its first major resurgence of measles since vaccination began in the 1960s. More than 50,000 cases occurred across three years when epidemiological models predicted that there should have been fewer than 9,000. The year after the Institute of Medicine's report was published, five healthy young people collapsed and died in the Southwestern U.S. from a hantavirus passed to them by deer mice. In 1996 researchers in Chicago discovered that antibiotic-resistant *Staphylococcus* bacteria had leapfrogged from their previous appearances in hospitals into everyday life, causing devastating illnesses in children who had no known risks for infection. Across health care, in urban life and in nature, decades of progress seemed to be breaking down.

"We forgot what rampant infectious disease looked like," says Katherine Hirschfeld, a professor of anthropology at the University of Oklahoma, who studies public health in failing states. "Science built us a better world, and then we got cocky and overconfident and decided we didn't have to invest in it anymore."

But unlike illnesses in the past–cholera epidemics in which the rich fled the cities, outbreaks of tuberculosis and plague blamed on immigrants, HIV cases for which gay men were stigmatized–infections of today do not arrive via easy scapegoats (although jingoistic politicians still try to create them). There is no type of place or person we can completely avoid; the globalization of trade, travel and population movement has made us all vulnerable. "We cannot divide the world anymore into countries that have dealt with infectious disease successfully and those that are still struggling," Hirschfeld says. "Countries have enclaves of great wealth and enclaves of poverty. Poor people work for rich people, doing their landscaping, making things in their factories. You cannot wall off risk."

The planet that slid down the far side of the 20th century's wave of confidence is the planet that enabled the spread of COVID. In the five years before its viral agent, SARS-CoV-2, began its wide travels, there were at least that many warnings that a globally emergent disease was due: the alerts appeared in academic papers, federal reports, think-tank war games and portfolios prepared at the White House to be handed off to incoming teams. The novel coronavirus slipped through known gaps in our defenses: it is a wildlife disease that was transmitted to humans by proximity and predation, spread by rapid travel, eased by insufficient surveillance, and amplified by nationalist politics and mutual distrust.

We were unprepared, with no vaccine or antiviral. In past epidemics of coronaviruses, such as SARS in 2003 and MERS in 2012, scientists had begun work on vaccines, but funding and interest dried up as the outbreaks waned. If research had continued, the emergency might have been shortened. Preventions and pharmaceuticals were the stellar achievements of the 20th century, but among scientists and physicians who deal with emerging diseases, there is a sense that attempts to repeat such successes will not be sufficient to save us. What is equally urgent, they argue, is attending to and repairing the conditions in which new diseases arise.

"Poverty has more impact than any of our technical interventions," says Peter J. Hotez, a physician and vaccine developer and founding dean of the Baylor University National School of Tropical Medicine. "Political collapse, climate change, urbanization, deforestation: these are what's holding us back. We can develop all the vaccines and drugs we want, but unless we figure out a way to deal with these other issues, we'll always be behind."

Evidence for Hotez's statement is abundant in the toll of those who suffered disproportionately in the COVID pandemic–people reliant on urban transit, living in public housing or nursing homes, or subject to the persistent effects of structural racism. What makes them vulnerable is never primarily a lack of drugs or vaccines. "My hospital is buried in COVID-19 patients," said infectious disease physician Brad Spellberg, chief medical officer at Los Angeles County–University of Southern California Medical Center, one of the largest public hospitals in the U.S., in mid-2020. "We serve a community of people who cannot physically distance. They are homeless, they are incarcerated, they are working poor living with a family of four in one room."

The term often used to denote what Hotez and Spellberg describe is "social determinants of health." It is an unsatisfying phrase that lacks the muscular directness of "shot" and "drug," but it is a crucial and also measurable concept: that social and economic factors, not just medical or innate immunological ones, strongly influence disease risk. Negative social determinants include unsafe housing, inadequate health care, uncertain employment and even a lack of political representation. They are the root cause of why the U.S., the richest country on Earth, has seen rising rates of hepatitis, sexually transmitted diseases, and parasitic and waterborne infections, as reported in *Scientific American* in 2018–infections that first arise among the poor and unhoused but then migrate to the wealthy and socially secure. As research by British epidemiologists Richard Wilkinson and Kate Pickett has shown, unequal societies are unhealthy ones: the larger the gap in income between a country's wealthiest and poorest, the more likely that country is to experience lower life expectancy and higher rates of chronic disease, teen births and infant mortality. That phenomenon goes a long way toward explaining why COVID wreaked such devastation in New York City, one of the most financially unequal cities in the country, before the city government applied the brute-force tool of lockdown and regained control.

Lockdowns are effective, but they cannot be sustained indefinitely, and they carry their own costs of severe mental health burdens and of keeping people from health care not related to the outbreak. And although quarantines may keep a pathogen from spreading for a while, they cannot stop a virus from emerging and finding a favorable human host. What might prevent or lessen that possibility is more prosperity more equally distributed–enough that villagers in South Asia need not trap and sell bats to supplement their incomes and that low-wage workers in the U.S. need not go to work while ill because they have no sick leave. An equity transition, if not an epidemiological one.

It is difficult to enumerate features of this more protected world without their sounding like a vague wish list: better housing, better income, better health care, better opportunities. Still, changes that some places around the globe enacted as defenses against COVID infection might make future infections less likely. Closing streets to encourage biking as Lisbon did, turning parking spaces into café spaces as happened in Paris, and creating broadband capacity for remote working and shifting health care to telemedicine, both done in the U.S.–these adaptations sound like technological optimism, but they could help us construct a society in which people need not crowd into unsafe urban spaces and in which income can be detached from geography.

It is certainly also necessary to re-up the investments in preparedness that the Institute of Medicine rebuked the U.S. for dropping almost 30 years ago. "We need to think about this with an insurance mindset," says Harvey Fineberg, a physician and president of the Gordon and Betty Moore Foundation, who was president of the institute when it prepared a 2003 follow-up to its warning. "If your house doesn't burn down, you don't bang your head on the wall on December 31 and say, Why did I buy that fire insurance? We buy insurance proactively to prevent the consequences of bad things that happen. That is the mindset we need to adopt when it comes to pandemics."

The U.S. responded to the coronavirus with an extraordinary, federally backed effort to find and test a vaccine in time to deliver 300 million doses by early 2021. This was a tremendous aspiration given that the shortest time in which a vaccine had ever been produced from scratch before then was four years (that vaccine was against mumps). There is no question that medical science is much better equipped than it was when Burnet was writing in the 1970s; *Natural History of Infectious Disease* came out before monoclonal antibody drugs, before gene therapy, before vaccines that could target cancers rather than microbes. The apotheosis of such work may be the development of chimeric antigen receptor T cell, or CAR-T, therapies, which debuted in 2017 and reengineer the body's own specialized immune system cells to combat cancers.

But CAR-T is also a sign of how concern for infectious diseases has slid into a trough of disregard. CAR-T therapies help a rare few patients at an extraordinary cost–their price before any insurance markup approaches 500,000 per infusion–whereas antibiotics, which have saved millions from death by infection, have slipped into peril. Most of the major companies that were making antibiotics in the 1970s–Eli Lilly, AstraZeneca, Bristol Myers Squibb and Novartis, among others–have left the sector, unable to make adequate profits on their products. In recent years at least six small biotechnology companies with new antibiotic compounds went bankrupt. This happened even though antibiotics are a crucial component of medicine–and some COVID patients have needed them to cure severe pneumonias that followed the initial viral infection.

Better structures for preparedness–disease surveillance, financial support for new drugs and vaccines, rapid testing, comprehensive reporting–will not by themselves get us to a planet safer from pandemics any more than car-free streets and inexpensive health care will. But they could give us a place from which to start, a position in which we are relatively more secure as a society, relatively more safe from known diseases, and more likely to detect previously unknown threats and to innovate in response to them.

Rosner, the historian, looks back to the explosive energy of the Progressive Era and wonders what a post-COVID equivalent might be. "In the 19th century we built entire water systems, we cleaned every street in cities," he says. "We have so constricted our vision of the world that it seems we can't address these issues. But there are moments in past crises when we have let the better angels in our society come to the fore: after the Great Depression, in the New Deal. It's not impossible."

About the Author

Maryn McKenna is a journalist specializing in public health, global health and food policy and a contributing editor at Scientific American. She is author of Big Chicken: The Incredible Story of How Antibiotics Created Modern Agriculture and Changed the Way the World Eats *(National Geographic Books, 2017).*

GLOSSARY

anatomy Study of elements and structure in the bodies of living beings.

anesthesia Insensitivity to pain, typically drug-induced for the purpose of surgery.

antibodies Blood proteins that form in response to specific pathogens to protect against them.

antisepsis Protection against the growth of microorganisms, especially in the context of surgery.

artery Blood vessels that deliver oxygen-rich blood to parts of the body.

cauterize To burn part of an injured body to prevent further bleeding or infection.

crescent A curved figure that tapers to two points.

diagnosis Formal identification of an illness, performed by a doctor following an examination of symptoms.

endemic Found in a particular area.

gibbet A structure for performing public executions.

gynecology A subset of medicine specifically focusing on reproductive biology for people who give birth.

Hippocratic Oath Traditional ethical guidelines for doctors, established by Hippocrates, an early pioneer of medicine.

inoculation The process of creating immunity to an illness by some exposure to it, whether via a vaccine or a mild form of the illness.

irascible Easily provoked to anger.

iron lung A large mechanical device that assisted in breathing, especially for polio survivors.

neuralgia A form of chronic pain appearing in the nerves.

pathogen An agent that causes illness.

peripatetic Frequently traveling from place to place.

physiology Study of the function of body parts; a companion to anatomy.

precocious Having developed abilities or talents at an unusually early point.

veins Blood vessels that return blood to the heart after delivering oxygen throughout the body.

yeoman Traditional term for a person who owned a small amount of land.

FURTHER INFORMATION

Centers for Disease Control and Prevention. "The Roots of Public Health and the CDC." www.cdc.gov/museum/online/story-of-cdc/roots/index.html.

Cohen, I. Bernard. "Florence Nightingale." *Scientific American*, March 1, 1984. www.scientificamerican.com/article/florence-nightingale/.

Fitzharris, Lindsey. "How Ether Transformed Surgery from a Race against the Clock." *Scientific American*, October 1, 2017. www.scientificamerican.com/article/how-ether-transformed-surgery-from-a-race-against-the-clock/.

Navarro, J. Alexander. "People Gave Up on Flu Pandemic Measures a Century Ago when They Tired of Them–and Paid a Price." *Scientific American*, March 26, 2021. www.scientificamerican.com/article/people-gave-up-on-flu-pandemic-measures-a-century-ago-when-they-tired-of-them-and-paid-a-price/.

Torjeson, Ingrid. "Drug Development: The Journey of a Medicine from Lab to Shelf." *The Pharmaceutical Journal*, May 12, 2015. pharmaceutical-journal.com/article/feature/drug-development-the-journey-of-a-medicine-from-lab-to-shelf.

Tucker, Holly. "Blood Lust: The Early History of Transfusion." *Scientific American*, July 12, 2011. www.scientificamerican.com/blog/guest-blog/blood-lust-the-early-history-of-transfusion/.

Yale Medicine Magazine Staff. "Medical Devices and Technology Across the Years." *Yale Medicine Magazine*, Summer 2019. medicine.yale.edu/news/yale-medicine-magazine/article/medical-devices-and-technology-across-the-years/.

CITATIONS

1.1 Galen by Frederick G. Kilgour (March 1, 1957); 2.1 Who Was Alessandra Giliani, 14th-Century Teen Anatomist? by Katie Hafner (July 12, 2023); 2.2 Vesalius: Discoverer of the Human Body by Martin Gumpert (May 1, 1948); 3.1 Hidden Black Scientists Proved the Polio Vaccine Worked by Ainissa Ramirez (June 17, 2021); 3.2 AIDS in 1988 by Robert C. Gallo ad Luc Montagnier (October 6, 2008); 3.3 Cures for Sickle Cell Disease Arrive After a Painful Journey by Maryn McKenna (September 17, 2024); 4.1 Ambroise Paré by Sir Geoffrey Keynes (January 1, 1956); 4.2 The Late Joseph Lister by John B. Huber (February 24, 1912); 5.1 The Medical Influence of the Stethoscope by Stanley Joel Reiser (February 1, 1979); 5.2 The Origins of Hypodermic Medication by Norman Howard-Jones (January 1, 1971); 6.1 Abortion and Contraception in the Middle Ages by Roland Betancourt (December 11, 2020); 6.2 The Forgotten History of the World's First Trans Clinic by Brandy Schillace (May 10, 2021); 6.3 The Disturbing History of Research into Transgender Identity by Jack Turban (October 23, 2020); 6.4 Commentary: The Eugenics Legacy of the Nobelist Who Fathered IVF by Osagie K. Obasogie (October 4, 2013); 7.1 Immunization against Smallpox before Jenner by William L. Langer (January 1, 1976); 7.2 What Florence Nightingale Can Teach Us about Architecture and Health by Steven Lockley (March 18, 2021); 7.3 We Learned the Wrong Lessons from the Tuskegee 'Experiment' by Melba Newsome (March 31, 2021); 7.4 In the Fight against Infectious Disease, Social Changes Are the New Medicine by Maryn McKenna (September 1, 2020).

Each author biography was accurate at the time the article was originally published.

INDEX

A

anatomy, 5, 7–9, 12, 15–18, 20–28, 30, 32, 37, 72–74, 76, 85–87, 92, 129
antibiotics, 62, 68, 144, 145, 147–149, 152, 153
antisepsis, 76, 77, 79, 103
Auenbrugger, Leopold, 84–87
avian flu, 145

B

bacteria, 41, 54, 78–80, 138, 145, 147, 149
bezoar, 73, 74
blood, 11, 12, 17, 23, 24, 30–37, 40, 44–46, 48–53, 55–59, 61, 65, 67, 71, 72, 78, 79, 93, 94, 98, 122, 138
British, 17, 50, 80, 95, 97, 98, 124, 129, 131, 151

C

cadavers, 15–17, 25, 35, 87
children, 39, 40, 43, 46, 55, 57, 58, 62–65, 68, 74, 77, 108, 109, 112, 116–124, 128–131, 135, 137, 144, 149
circadian rhythm, 139, 140
clinical trials, 41, 58, 65, 142, 143
COVID-19, 140, 142, 143, 145, 149–151, 153
cowpox, 136, 137

D

death, 7, 10, 12, 16, 18, 20, 28–30, 42, 61, 62, 71–77, 96, 107, 109, 111, 115, 128, 130, 131, 132, 134–136, 141, 143, 145, 147, 148
dissection, 9, 15, 16, 22–26, 74
DNA, 44, 45, 51, 57

E

epidemic, 9, 39, 44, 50, 51, 52, 55, 56, 128, 131, 133, 134, 139, 144–146, 148–150

F

flu, 144, 145
French, 46, 47, 50, 56, 70, 72, 73, 83, 93–96, 112, 132–134

G

Galen, 5, 7–13, 21, 23–26, 32–34, 36
gender, 112–120
genes, 44, 45, 49–51, 57–59, 62, 63, 65–68, 114, 115, 123–126, 152

Greek, 7, 23, 32, 70, 74, 78, 83, 85, 93, 100, 109, 129

H

health care, 62, 66, 112, 120, 143, 149, 151, 153
HeLa cells, 40–43
Hippocrates, 8, 11, 21, 75, 106
Hippocratic Oath, 106, 107
Hirschfeld, Magnus, 111–116, 149

I

infectious, 44–46, 77, 79, 128, 144–150, 152
injection, 39, 43, 93–104, 141

J

Jenner, Edward, 128, 129, 136, 137

L

Lister, Joseph, 21, 76, 77, 79–81, 103

M

muscles, 9, 10, 17, 25, 26, 34, 63

N

natural light, 138, 140
nerves, 9, 10–12, 22, 24, 50, 80, 93, 96–99, 101

P

pandemic, 140, 144–146, 150, 152, 153
penicillin, 62, 141, 144
polio, 39–41, 43, 144, 147
publications, 8, 12, 20, 21, 23–25, 28, 30, 31, 33, 61, 67, 74, 75, 85–87, 89, 91, 94, 97–99, 101–104

R

racism, 66, 143, 150
retrovirus, 44–49, 49, 54, 56
Roman, 8, 20, 22, 70, 109

S

Salk, Jonas, 39–41, 43, 144
scars, 60, 128, 136
sepsis, 79
smallpox, 79, 128–137, 144, 147
specimens, 25, 47
surgery, 5, 10, 22, 23, 27, 37, 60, 70–72, 74–77, 79–81, 103, 106, 108, 109, 113, 114, 116

T

Tuskegee, 40–43, 141, 142

V

vaccines, 5, 39–41, 43, 44, 50, 54–56, 94, 136, 137, 141–144, 147, 148, 150, 152, 153
variolation, 129–133, 135, 136
veins, 9, 11, 12, 22, 23, 30, 32–34, 36, 37

Vesalius, 12, 20–29, 32, 70, 74, 85
viruses, 39, 40, 41, 44, 54, 138, 141, 142, 145, 148–152

X

X-rays, 91, 92